LIV
on the
FRINGE
of the
MOB

JOSEPH P. O'DONNELL
AS TOLD BY
E. STEVEN SACHS

outskirts
press

DEDICATION

*To two very special men in my life who sadly
passed away before this book was published:*

*My father-in-law, David Gorkin: World War II veteran
(Army Air Force), a kind, wonderful man, and a voracious
reader who consumed every word of my manuscripts and
whose encouragement inspired me to continue writing.*

*My uncle, Lenny Tauber: World War II veteran (Army)
and a charismatic, generous person with whom I spent
many enjoyable hours discussing history, sports, politics
and life, in general. Like the main subject of this book,
he conducted a very successful, legitimate business
while nevertheless maintaining close friendships with
men who were connected to the New York Mob.*

Joseph P. O'Donnell

Table of Contents

Foreword

Most people have heard or read stories about the Mafia, commonly known as "the Mob." Some of the most popular and award-winning movies—classics for sure—have been devoted to the inner workings of the Mob—the family connections, involvement with criminal activities, control of politicians, and many aspects of everyday life in America. To say that we, as a society, are fascinated with the Mob is an understatement.

My relationship with members of the Mob, however, was very different from what you can imagine.

All my experiences were legitimate, business-like, and characterized by mutual respect. Some relationships were deeply personal and most enjoyable. I was never asked to do anything illegal, and if I had been, I never would have done so.

As a young boy in Brooklyn, I grew up and played with some kids who ultimately became major figures in the Mob. We forged friendships and a bond that carried over to adulthood. I always understood how these men evolved from the streets of Brooklyn, New York City, and the Bronx to lofty positions of power and influence.

I never questioned how they made money or conducted their lives.

I never asked why they had such bad reputations.

As I grew older, I made contacts and developed business relationships and friendships with other major figures in the Mob. On numerous occasions my family and I were invited to their homes for dinner, especially around Christmas and other holidays.

I enjoyed their company, and they always made me feel welcome.

I grew up and flourished during a time when the meat industry was one of the most corrupt in America. There were times when I could have been drawn in, formed a partnership with my competitors, and gotten caught up in business dealings that were illegal. In those situations I could have easily called on my family of friends in the Mob to intervene on my behalf—to put pressure on my competitors to back off and leave me alone. Better yet, to take over a customer or contract they already owned. But that intervention could have gotten out of hand, with someone being injured or worse. Then I could have been the center of a criminal investigation.

But I was lucky.

I stood my ground, resisted the temptation, and remained independent.

My friends in the Mob knew I could have asked for their "muscle."

I never did.

Because of this fierce independence, I gained the respect not only of those in the meat industry, but also of my friends in the Mob.

Since those days, most of the individuals in this book have passed on. In many cases I have changed or omitted their names out of respect for them and their surviving families.

I'll leave it to your imagination to figure out who they might have been.

CHAPTER 1

The Tombs

I WAS ARRESTED at five o'clock in the morning and taken to The Tombs, the common name for the Manhattan Detention Complex—New York's most historic jail. They told me I would be held there until my court appearance the next day.

This building was the third edition of the original jail that was built in 1835 in an Egyptian Revival style of architecture. Because of its eerie appearance, it resembled a Pharaoh's tomb, and its nickname and reputation quickly became fixed in the lexicon of New York discourse. If someone heard you were taken to The Tombs, they knew you were screwed. This was as true in the 1960s as it was in 1835. A lot of tough guys ended up in The Tombs, and some of them learned the hard way that they weren't so tough after all.

The original building was torn down in the early 1900s only to be rebuilt in a Gothic Revival style. Then in 1936 that building was demolished, and a new Deco/Modern building was erected across the street on Centre Street. (1)

Despite these architectural and location changes, nothing about The Tombs really changed, including its nickname. A prisoner being held in The Tombs could end up dead before his lawyer could ever get him to stand before a judge.

Two guards pulled me by my shackled arms toward a large door that opened into a room known as The Hole. The heavy shackles around my ankles caused me to stumble as I tried to keep pace with their long, rapid strides.

What's their hurry, or is this just a way for the guards to inflict their own measure of punishment?

Sweat dripped off my grimy face, and I felt ripples of blood trickling down from several cuts and scratches on my forehead and cheeks.

My lower lip was swollen.

My clothes were muddied and torn.

Simply stated, I was a mess.

When we reached the large door, the first guard leaned down to undo my leg shackles.

The second guard—a burly guy with a large, flabby beer gut that hung over his belt buckle—moved closer and looked at me with a sarcastic sneer. "Welcome back to The Tombs, Sachs. You must like it here. You're makin' visits to this place a real habit," he said.

I stared back at him and said nothing.

The first guard unlocked the large door and keyed open my arm shackles while the second guard applied a firm grasp to my shoulders. In one coordinated motion, the first guard then opened the large door while the second guard shoved me into The Hole.

"Get in there, asshole!" the second guard yelled.

I lost my balance, stumbled through the doorway, and fell to the floor.

The door slammed behind me.

I heard a metallic click as the lock was reset and then the sound of the guards laughing as they walked away.

I got to my feet and looked around.

The room was crowded with approximately sixty men, a few sitting on one large bench and the others sitting on the floor, some on newspapers quietly talking, while others were curled up sound asleep. The left corner of the room had an open toilet, basically a hole in the ground.

The room reeked of human body odor and excrement.

My clumsy entrance into the room had failed to garner any attention. None of the men even looked up at me.

One huge Black man, about six feet, four inches tall and no less than three hundred and fifty pounds was stretched out on the only other bench on the far-right side of the room with his head resting on a folded towel. The fact that he had the bench all to himself spoke volumes about his position within the group of criminals. He was clearly their leader, someone with whom to be reckoned.

I took a deep breath and continued to survey the men in the room.

The only white face in the entire holding area was mine.

A white Jewish guy in a room with sixty black and Latino criminals?

I knew right away that I had to show strength, not fear, if I was going to come out of the room alive.

I walked through the crowded room, stepping over and around the men on the floor. I headed to the large man stretched out alone on the bench.

I leaned down and pushed firmly on his shoulder.

"Move over," I said.

The murmuring and chatter in the room became silent.

Dead silence.

All eyes in the room were suddenly focused on me.

The large man looked up at me. "You are either crazy or good." He slowly swung his legs toward the floor, sat up, and slid over to one side of the bench. He continued to stare at me with a menacing look.

"I am good," I said, as I sat down beside him.

A few seconds passed.

"What's your name, brother?" I asked.

"Tiny."

"Good name for a big guy like you."

I closed my eyes and feigned drifting off.

A few seconds later an elbow jabbed into my rib cage. "Whaddya arrested for?" Tiny asked.

"Assault and battery."

I closed my eyes again.

Another elbow jolted my rib cage. "Assault on who?"

"Cops. Tenth Precinct. Resisting arrest."

Tiny looked at me and smiled. "Those Tenth Precinct ass-holes deserve a little resistance now and then. Did you hurt one of 'em?"

"Not sure. Three cops stepped in to help the first cop that tried to cuff me. By the time I got done with them, they were covered with blood, some of it mine, some of it theirs. I couldn't tell how bad they were hurt."

Tiny stared at me with a blank look for a few seconds. His mouth dropped open. Then he broke out into loud laughter. "Look at this dude! Beats the shit out of those 10th Precinct cops and then joins our party here in The Hole!"

His fellow gang members, who had sat quietly, seemingly stunned by my aggressive approach to their leader, took his cue and joined in the frivolity.

The walls rocked with laughter.

A few of Tiny's gang members walked over to our bench to slap me on the shoulder or hit my hand with a high-five.

Two of the guards looked in through the horizontal peep

holes to see what the hell was going on.

A few minutes later the door opened and a long table was wheeled into the room. The tabletop had two stacks of sliced white bread, two piles of bologna, a bowl filled with liverwurst, and two pitchers—one filled with milk, the other with hot tea.

Nothing looked appetizing to me.

Tiny slapped me on the back. "Come on, my friend. Let's have some breakfast," he said.

We got up and walked over to the table.

"I'm not hungry. You want an extra sandwich?" I asked.

"Sure thing, my friend," he said as he loaded his plate.

I didn't tell him that a Jewish guy never ate liverwurst and bologna, no matter how hungry he might be. Besides, I had no interest in filling up on food and drink and then needing to use that open toilet while sixty guys stared at me.

Fourteen hours later my lawyer showed up and I was released from The Tombs.

I had become a target of the cops from the crooked Tenth Precinct. They were in the back pockets of the drug dealers as well as some rogue members of the Mob, which is why I had been roughed up and arrested.

My lawyer informed me that my friend, Jack Peace—the captain of the New York Police Department in my precinct, the Midtown South—had made a phone call to the captain of the Tenth Precinct and told him to drop the charges.

But that's a whole other story.

CHAPTER 2

Growing Up

Ages eight through fourteen

I FOUGHT MY way all through my childhood.

I'm not sure whether I had to prove something to the other kids or if I had to prove it to myself. Whatever the motivation, those years laid the foundation for the toughness I needed to get through a very complicated life.

In 1949 I was eight years old and my parents moved to the Woodhaven section of Brooklyn commonly known as the Asshole End, located right on the border of Queens—South Ozone Park. I was the only Jewish kid within miles. Most of the families were Italian, Irish, or German, a real mix, except for the lack of other Jewish families.

I was singled out as different—the Jew. Being the only Jewish kid on the block certainly didn't help my relationship with other kids in my neighborhood as well as those who lived in other areas. Initially this fact bothered me, but it was a distinction I learned to deal with.

Twice a week I had to walk more than twenty blocks through some tough neighborhoods to get to Hebrew school. The kids in those areas spotted me and yelled out, "Hey, there goes the Jew. Let's get him!"

I had to tuck my Hebrew books under my belt and run like hell to get away from them. Some days there could be ten kids chasing me. If they caught me, I had to fight my way out of their grasp. I learned how to defend myself, and in doing so, I took a hefty toll on my opponents. I bloodied more noses and dished out more black eyes than I received, and the balance of that equation wasn't even close.

Nevertheless, I never forgot those attacks and the beatings I received. I vowed to get even with those kids someday.

Back in my neighborhood I became friends with the kids who lived in my area and played with them. We played the usual games—baseball, stick ball, basketball, football—but the games I remember most are those that we never saw in a ball-park, gym, or arena.

We played triangle "stoop ball," and, after it got dark, one of my favorites, "kick the can." The object in the game was to kick the can and then run the bases before the kid who retrieved the can could tag you out. The problem was that we used old number ten cans with jagged edges. A few times we had to run for help to call an ambulance because one of the kids got cut so deeply on the head, hand, or a leg that we couldn't stop the bleeding.

Another great game was Ringo-Levio, in which one team of kids covered their eyes for a specified count while the others hid. The team that covered their eyes then searched for the other team members until they were found, "captured," and put in "jail," often simply a bench, a stoop, or a space between two parked cars. The game was over when all the captured players were put in jail. However, if one of the hiding players broke free from his hiding place and barged into the jail without being caught, he could free all his teammates by tagging them and shouting, "Home! Free all," which meant that all members that were in jail were free and had to be caught again. (2)

The only problem that I caused in this game was that I used to hide in garbage cans. No one ever caught me.

I'd go home smelling like fish, and my mother and father would ask, "Where the hell have you been?"

While I was in elementary school, I'm not sure if I found the fights or the fights found me, before school, lunch time, after school; it didn't seem to matter. Some days I had three fights before I got home.

By the time I got to high school at Franklin K. Lane, I had become one of the best street fighters in Brooklyn, but I took some pretty good licks along the way, and my mother got tired of patching me up almost every day.

One day after one of my fights, I was bleeding from the mouth, nose, and eye—every facial orifice. My mother was tending to my wounds when we heard the doorbell ring. She stopped for a few seconds and went to the door.

A small group of my "friends" stood in the doorway. Jimmy Ripp stepped forward and spoke for the group. "Sorry to bother you, Mrs. Sachs, but there's a gang up on Crescent Street that's after us. We need Steve's help."

"What do you want from him?" my mother cried. "He's still bleeding, for Chrissakes!"

"We know," said Jimmy Ripp. "But he's one of the best street fighters around, and we need him to help us."

My mother shook her head in exasperation, closed the door, and walked over to the chair where I sat. She finished applying my bandages without saying a word, and then she looked at me sternly. "Go to your room," she said. "This is one street fight you'll have to sit out."

Jimmy Ripp was a beauty. My mother used to call him Jack the Ripper. He loved playing with cherry bombs. Sometimes he'd throw them, and when they hit something, they exploded with a loud boom. One time he actually threw one at a gasoline truck. Luckily that one didn't explode. Many years later I heard that Jimmy Ripp developed neurological issues and ended up in a mental hospital.

I wasn't surprised.

CHAPTER 3

The Streetfighter

MY TECHNIQUE IN street fighting was a bit unusual; perhaps that's why it was so successful. First of all, I almost never threw the first punch. I didn't want to be characterized as an aggressor, a trouble-making guy who started fights. Rather I preferred the reputation of a reactor, a guy who didn't take shit from anyone and a person who responded to an aggressor by taking him down like he had never been taken down before.

Early on I noticed that when a guy threw a punch at me, he expected that I would respond with a punch of my own. His attention was therefore entirely fixed on my hands, hoping to block any of my punches directed at him, so I surprised him with a sharp and powerful leg kick directed squarely at his balls.

Over the years that I was involved in street fighting, I was amazed at how effective the direct-to-the-balls method worked and how few of my opponents saw it coming. Some of them literally dropped to their knees in pain, their arms, hands, and fists useless to respond.

Once the asshole was immobilized, I followed up with a slashing back-handed forearm thrust to the side of the neck. Occasionally this blow landed directly on the Adam's apple, causing my victim to keel over coughing, retching, and choking for air.

If there was still resistance, I finished him off with a right cross to the side of the face.

I was quick as lightning; all this punishment could be meted out in a matter of five seconds or less. I soon garnered the respect of my friends who often re-told the stories of my fights to each other, almost reveling in the glorious way I took some guy down. As time went on, the factual details became embellished to the point that the incident itself became a fictitious creation bearing little similarity to the original confrontation.

I didn't care. I enjoyed having the respect that came with the legend.

As I got older—age twelve to thirteen—my friends decided to form a crew, some younger guys, some older guys, for the purpose of creating a group identity that would link us to our neighborhood. They flipped the name of our section from Woodhaven to Havenwood. We became known as The Havenwood AC. The "AC" was supposed to mean Athletic Club, but we were into gang fights more than sports.

We had a formidable group—real tough, street-smart guys: Lenny Grasso, Tommy Failla, Jimmy Ripp, the Lanoue twins, JG, and a couple of the Gambino boys.

One day JG suggested that we jump on our bikes and ride up to Jamaica Avenue to buy bows and arrows to take to Forest Park Cemetery for rabbit hunting. On the way we crossed paths with another gang of kids under the Jamaica El. They stopped and stared at us, sizing up the newcomers that had entered their territory.

We could have just ridden by and not said a word, but JG would have none of that. He provoked them, as only he could. "You guys live in this rat hole?" he yelled.

The leader of the other gang yelled back, "You better get the fuck out of here."

"We're not going anywhere," said JG. "We're stayin' right here and we're gonna kick your asses."

JG was one of us, so we stood with him shoulder to shoulder.

The other gang members took notice and gathered right next to their leader.

Next thing we knew, we were in the middle of a rumble. Lots of swearing. Fists flying. Blood splattering. A few teeth were knocked out. Some kids needed stitches.

In the end we won the fight, but still came home battered and bruised. We never made it to Forest Park Cemetery.

It turned out to be a good day for the rabbits.

CHAPTER 4

Meeting the Young Bonannos and Colombos

BY THE TIME I was twelve years old I had been in too many fights and had gotten into too much trouble in the neighborhood where we lived. My mother thought I needed a change of scenery and decided to send me to my two cousins' house every Saturday morning. They lived on Carroll and Presidents streets in Brooklyn, not far from Eastern Parkway.

My father planned to drop me off on Carroll Street early on Saturday mornings as he drove to work in New York City.

My cousins, Billy and Paul, were fifteen. Their friends—Tony, Butchie, Joey, Dominick, and Sally—were also either fifteen or sixteen. They had a club in my cousins' basement on Carroll Street where they got together to lift weights, smoke cigarettes, and talk about girls.

This was my first exposure to the Bonannos and Colombos. They were built like linebackers—a very tough bunch.

On the first Saturday, my cousin Paul took care of my introduction. "Hey guys, this is our cousin, Stevie. He's only twelve, but he's a tough kid … a heck of a street fighter. He's gonna be comin' over every Saturday to hang out with us."

The other four kids paid little attention and said nothing, and then one of the Bonannos spoke up and asked, "You been laid yet, kid?"

"Cut it out, Joey. Leave 'm alone," said Paul.

Not knowing what to say, I stood quietly, just grateful that my cousin had intervened and bailed me out.

Eventually I was a welcomed member of the group and became a regular Saturday guest. Sometimes a few of their girlfriends came over to visit when my aunt and uncle were not at home.

The boys convinced Aunt Mary that they needed to lie down on a mattress in between weightlifting workouts. She actually fell for that story and got a used mattress that was placed in the basement near the workout area.

My mother thought she was getting me away from trouble. She had no idea about the education I got on Saturdays.

Two years later my parents moved us to Far Rockaway on Bay 25th Street across from the high school. It was primarily a Jewish neighborhood, and I became friends with an entirely new group—Barry Kramer, Murray Loecher, and Dave Sandlofer. The four of us—all Jewish—had a good time together that summer, and as a result, became a very tight crew. Two weeks before school started, we decided to go bowling at the famous Falcaro's Bowling Lanes on Peninsula Boulevard in Inwood. My three new friends had bicycles; I did not, so I hopped on the back of Dave's bike, and we pedaled about five miles to Falcaro's.

While we were bowling, a group of five guys wearing black, purple, and gray jackets—the symbol of the Lucky Seven gang—started to bowl on a lane near us. Apparently they knew Dave, and one guy shouted over to him, "Hey, Jew boy, you trying to bowl?"

I didn't need to hear anything more. "Hey, watch your big

mouth, or I'll close it for you," I shouted back.

Dave immediately mumbled into my ear, "Those guys are Lucky Seven. You don't want to start anything with them." He then stepped in front of me and yelled over, "Sorry. We're okay here."

The blond-haired leader of the group stepped toward us. "Well, we're not okay here. Tell your friend over there that he better keep his fuckin' mouth shut or we're gonna kick the shit out of him."

I pushed Dave aside gently and stepped forward to confront my new aggressor. "Anytime you're ready, pal," I said.

The manager of the bowling alley heard the commotion and rushed over to stand between us. "Hey, guys, no fighting in here. Take your disagreement outside or I'm calling the cops," he said. He started to walk away but suddenly turned around as if struck by an important thought. "And take your bowling shoes off and turn them in at the counter before you leave. You're done for the day."

We reluctantly sat down on the bench and changed our shoes. I looked over at the Lucky Seven group of five. They were doing the same.

Four against five, I thought to myself. *Still no problem. I've faced tougher odds.*

We walked outside to the parking lot. Within seconds the leader of Lucky Seven came over and got in my face. His four friends stood behind him, ready to jump in for support.

"You better get the fuck out of here and never come back," the leader yelled.

I didn't waste any time. I cold-cocked him with a hammer-like right cross to the left side of his face.

Stunned, he went down to the ground in a heap. He coughed once and then spit out a tooth.

One down, four to go. Now we're evened up.

But my mathematical analysis was way off. In a flash my three friends hopped on their bikes and took off.

I was left alone.

Four against one—much more than I bargained for. This calls for more drastic action.

I immediately took off my Garrison belt, a thick leather belt with a big buckle so sharp it could cut. I wrapped it around my wrist and started swinging it around wildly.

As the four guys closed in on me, I caught one of them on his face. Blood splattered everywhere. He let out a painful scream, grabbed at his face, saw the blood, and ran back inside the bowling alley for help.

Now three against one, I was forced to retreat to a more defensive position.

Traffic on Peninsula Boulevard was backed up at a traffic light. I turned around and began darting between and around the stopped cars as I tried to evade the three attackers.

A man in an open-air Jeep spotted me and called out, "Hey, son, you need a ride?"

With that, I jumped into his Jeep.

The light changed, and he floored it, tires screeching as he raced toward Cedarhurst and Central Avenue, leaving the three kids far behind and totally bewildered.

"What was that all about?" he asked.

"The leader of a Lucky Seven gang was making fun of my friend, so I punched him out and the rest of the gang came after me."

"Where's your friend?"

"He got scared and took off with my other friends."

"And left you alone?"

"Yeah."

"Some friends you have there." He shook his head and laughed. He drove for a few more minutes and then dropped me off at the bus station. "You good from here?" he asked.

"Yeah, I'm okay."

I took a bus to Far Rockaway and walked home from the bus station on Central Avenue. As I moved along the street, I slipped my belt though the loops in my jeans. The blood on the buckle had dried.

I left it there.

CHAPTER 5

The Gang War I Almost Caused

A FEW DAYS later I met up with my three "friends" who had abandoned me and forced me to take on Lucky Seven by myself. They looked uneasy, eyes darting back and forth to each other. They obviously did not know what to say.

I assumed they were just nervous and somewhat embarrassed by their gutless performance in the face of adversity, especially when I, as a new friend, had stepped up to defend one of them from an anti-Semitic bully.

Their behavior was strange, and I couldn't figure out why.

Two weeks later, when I began my sophomore year in high school, it all became clear to me. While I was eating in the school cafeteria, two of the biggest senior football players came over to my table.

At five feet ten inches tall, I was a pretty big guy myself, but those guys towered over me.

"Are you Steve Sachs?" one of them asked.

"Yes. Who wants to know?"

"We need to talk to you."

"About what?"

"It's better if we talk outside."

The first guy turned and walked toward the back door of

the cafeteria that led to the football field. The second guy motioned for me to follow him. As I walked toward the door, all the other kids in the cafeteria stared at me. A few whispered to their friends. Some had their mouths open as if they were about to witness a historic event.

How come everyone here seems to know what's going on except me?

We got outside. The two big guys flanked me, one on each side.

I looked around.

There was no one else on the football field.

Am I going to fight these two guys alone? If so, I'm ready.

I looked into the stands. At least another twenty guys were sitting there, all mumbling to each other while motioning toward me. Suddenly a short blond-haired kid stood up and began walking down the steps of the grandstand toward me. The other group of twenty followed right behind him, their apparent leader.

I was clearly a target and still had no idea why.

I was not the type to lie back and cower in the face of an aggressor, though, so I took the initiative and began walking toward him. As I got closer, I could see a smirk on his face.

What does this kid know that I don't know?

We stopped less than a foot away from each other.

"I'm Jimmy Pulis," he said.

"Am I supposed to know you?"

"I live in Rockaway Beach on 100th Street. Irishtown."

"Okay, but why is that important to me?"

"Because my crew, including my three brothers, have been fighting with Lucky Seven for two years."

"Sorry to hear that. I've had my own problems with Lucky Seven."

"Yeah. I know all about it."

"How's that?" I asked.

"Because a few weeks ago you beat the shit out of the younger brother of the leader of Lucky Seven."

"He's a punk with a big mouth and came after me. What was I supposed to do, be nice to him?"

"You knocked out a couple of his teeth."

I smiled. "Was that all?" I asked.

"Then you cut up another's kid's face. He needed stitches. Might end up with a few scars."

I resisted the urge to look down at my belt buckle. "True, but it started out as five against one. What would you have done, lie down and let them beat you to a pulp?"

He paused for a few seconds and looked away, seemingly processing my line of logic. He then stepped closer. "What you don't know is that last month we made a truce with Lucky Seven. No more gang fights. And then you come along and beat up the leader's younger brother. So now they think we sent you over there." He inched even closer, nose-to-nose with me. "You just started a fuckin' gang war."

I didn't flinch. I just stood there and didn't back away. "Wasn't my fault. They started it," I said.

He laughed.

"Okay, well now you're gonna have to help us finish it. We'll pick you up Saturday night on your street at seven o'clock. You better be ready."

"Ready for what?"

"We're meeting with Lucky Seven in the fields behind Lawrence High School to see if the truce holds or whether we have a gang fight. Or we might just let you and the younger brother duke it out."

I turned and started to walk away, heading back toward the

door that entered the school. I walked "strong," as I always did, head up, shoulders back, showing confidence and especially no fear.

"Don't worry. I'm always ready. See you Saturday night," I said.

Jimmy Pulis stood there and said nothing.

I never looked back at him but caught his reflection in the large glass window of the cafeteria. He studied me all the way to the door.

A few days passed. It seemed like a month.

I wasn't nervous in the least, but there was a certain level of anticipation that occupied my mind every hour of every day.

On Saturday night at seven p.m. I was picked up by Jimmy Pulis and a few other kids. Together we had a caravan of six different beat-up cars that drove over to the field behind Lawrence High School. The two groups assembled on the field as if preparing for a hockey face-off—Lucky Seven on one side and the Irishtown gang on the other.

Jimmy Pulis spoke to one of the Lucky Seven for a few minutes and then walked back to me. "The brother doesn't want to take you on again," he said.

I shrugged. "I'm not surprised. Now what?" I asked.

Suddenly we heard sirens and saw the flashing blue lights of police cars headed toward the field. We bolted toward the parked cars in a frantic effort to get away. I hopped into one of the cars, and we drove out of the field before any of the cops could catch us.

I found out later that a few kids got nabbed by the cops, but no charges were brought against them. Since no fighting had broken out, no one had done anything wrong. Outside of a few knives and some baseball bats, none of which were illegal, no weapons were confiscated.

On Monday morning I happened to meet Jimmy Pulis in the hallway of the high school in between classes.

"Hey, Sachs. I worked it out with Lucky Seven. The truce is still in effect."

"That's good news for you but doesn't affect me at all."

He laughed. "Oh, but it does."

"How so? I'm not a member of your crew. What happens with your guys and Lucky Seven is none of my business."

His tone turned serious as he issued a harsh warning. "Look, Sachs, you better take your Brooklyn attitude and stick it up your ass. Any comments you make to a Lucky Seven member must be cleared with me first. I can't have you starting any more problems."

I walked closer to him to make sure my response was perfectly clear. "I'll do what I want to do and say what I want to say to anyone at the time I feel like saying it. And no one, especially you, is going to tell me what to do." I turned and headed down the hallway to my next class.

I never talked to Jimmy Pulis again.

CHAPTER 6

The Colonel

IN LATE 1960 I was enrolled part-time at New York University and thinking about getting married. Despite this post-World War II peacetime period, there was considerable talk from Washington about the need to expand the nation's military.

I was concerned about my draft status and, if drafted, being required to go into the Army full-time for two years. I heard about a program that allowed one to fulfill his military obligation through a six-month training period followed by six years in the National Guard. I applied to the program but was informed that it was closed.

Uncle Joe, my mother's brother-in-law, was a lawyer and also ran a textile business. He was a very loving individual who always went out of his way to help a family member. He heard about my dilemma and suggested that I call a contact, Colonel Paul Miller, who was located at the Marine Parkway Naval Base. My uncle said he had heard that Colonel Miller was in charge of the six-month program.

The next day I called the colonel while I was at the Topps plant.

To my surprise he answered the phone himself.

I identified myself and wasted no time getting right to the

point. "Sir, I'm interested in signing up for the six-month training program but was told it was closed."

A deep, clear voice came through the phone. "Yes, it is, but I may be able to help," he said. He paused for a second and then asked, "By any chance are you free now?"

"Sure."

"Great. Then why don't you come down to my house and meet with me and my son." He gave some quick directions, and within fifteen minutes I was cleaned up and ready to leave the office.

My father was sitting at his desk as I walked by. "Where the hell are you going?" he asked.

"I'm going to see an Army recruiter."

"Army recruiter? Are you kidding? There's a fuckin' war going on, and you want to join the Army?"

"Uncle Joe recommended a colonel who can get me into the reserves so I won't get drafted."

"Oh yeah, that'll work until they activate your reserve unit. Then you'll be duckin' your head in a rice paddy while the Viet Cong are shooting at you. Nice fuckin' plan you have there."

I was ripping mad. His usual insulting attitude had gotten the best of me. "Look," I said. "I'm twenty years old. I can make my own decisions. Besides, I'm thinking about getting married."

"Married? Another stupid decision."

"You never quit, do you? You're on my case all day long. I bust my ass for your company every day, but you never give me even a minute of respect or appreciation. Mom is right about you. You're a mean, self-centered bastard."

Now he was pissed. "Don't bring your mother into this," he said.

"Why not? You treat her even worse than you treat me."

He dismissed my comment with a wave of his hand. "She

knows nothing. You should look at things the way I do."

"The way you do? Like cheating the government on your taxes? Or adding filler to the hamburger meat to increase your profits? I don't ever want to be like you." I was furious, but I wasn't finished venting. I walked over to the office door, stopped abruptly, and turned toward my father. "And one more thing," I said. "I've got news for you. One of these days Mom's gonna leave you, and when she does, she'll end up owning half of this place."

I walked out of the office and slammed the door behind me.

These conversations—perhaps better-stated as confrontations—between my father and me had become commonplace, and over time, as you will see, they actually deteriorated even further. On that day, however, I maintained my focus and proceeded, undeterred, to my appointment.

The colonel's house was located in the town of Arverne, not far from Far Rockaway. I drove by an elementary school, turned right past a small schoolyard, and turned right again at a street with a stretch of row houses of Cape Cod design that faced the schoolyard. In between every two to three houses there was an alleyway that led to a parking area in the back. I turned into the alleyway next to the colonel's house, drove to the back, and parked my car. I had hardly walked up the steps when the door to the house opened.

A tall broad-shouldered man stood in the doorway. "You must be Steve," he said.

"Yes, sir, nice to meet you," I said as I reached out and shook his hand.

He invited me in and led me to his office to the side of the living room. A tall, skinny young guy stood up as we entered.

"Steve," the colonel said, "This is my son, Robert. He helps me with the six-month program you're interested in."

We sat down, exchanged a few more pleasantries, and then I explained my situation and my interest in the six-month program.

The colonel wasted no time getting down to business. "As you know, Steve, the six-month program is closed. The physical capacity has been reached and the Army is not accepting any more applicants. However, I can pull a few strings and get you on the roster if you are serious about enrolling," he said.

"Definitely," I said. "It's the perfect program for my school and work schedule right now. And, besides, I'm thinking about getting married."

"That's great," he said. "Just great." Then he paused for a few seconds and leaned back on his swivel club chair. He tapped a pencil lightly on a yellow notepad on the front of his desk. It seemed like he was formulating a plan before speaking. "You know, Steve," he started. "Making the arrangements to enroll someone in a program that's already closed can be very time-consuming and challenging. You have to speak to the right people, overcome a lot of obstacles, get by all the red tape. You know what I mean, right?"

"Sure," I said. "Must take a lot of work." I resisted the temptation to say, "And you have to pay off the right people."

But the colonel and I were on the same wavelength. His next comments didn't surprise me in the least.

"So we're looking at a pretty costly deal here."

"How costly?" I asked.

"Fourteen hundred dollars."

In 1960 that was a lot of money. But I didn't flinch. I simply reached into my back pocket and took out my wallet. Fortunately I had gotten my two-week cash payment for working in my father's meat plant.

The colonel looked surprised and darted a quick glance

toward his son. His son nodded to him. Then the colonel quickly looked back at me.

Their body language looked suspicious to me, but I just shrugged it off as I counted the money out on the desk.

"I've got seven hundred in cash here," I said. "And I can bring the other seven hundred in two weeks." I reached across the desk and dropped the money in front of the colonel.

With huge smiles on their faces, the colonel and his son got up from their chairs, shook my hand vigorously, and led me back to the door.

In some ways I felt like I may have just made a pact with the devil, but I needed that program and figured that guy—a high-ranking military officer—knew how to get me into it.

As I left the house, I glanced up to the deck three houses away and saw two men standing there. One of them seemed to be holding a camera. I paid no further attention to them as I hurried down the staircase, proceeded to my car, and drove away.

Two weeks later I drove back to the colonel's house. Once again I was welcomed with a big greeting by the colonel. His son was not present at the second meeting.

"Have a seat, Steve," he said. "Good to see you again."

"Same here, sir."

He wasted no more time and got right to the point. "Were you able to come up with the rest of the money?"

"Yes, no problem. But first I've got a couple of questions."

"Of course, whatever you need to know."

"Tell me a little more about the training. When does it start? What's involved?"

He sat up in his chair, swallowed hard, and waved his right hand as if brushing my questions aside. "Oh, don't worry about the training. I'll sign you in every month. You don't even have to show up."

I stared over at him in disbelief. "What? Don't worry about the training? I want the training. It's part of the program I'm paying to get into. What kind of bullshit is this?"

He reached out toward me, practically pleading. "Calm down, calm down. I've got you covered. You can devote more time to your night classes and your job—"

I cut him off mid-sentence.

"Covered? You can't cover this. It sounds illegal to me, and I don't want any part of it. Give my fuckin' money back to me before I report this." I was steaming, nearly out of control.

He sized up the situation and took on an apologetic tone. "No problem," he said. "I'll get your money back to you in a week."

I turned away and started walking toward the door. "Call me when you have the cash, and I'll be here." I stormed out the door. I was furious at the thought that I had been scammed. As I walked down the stairs, some movement on the staircase of the school directly across the street caught my eye. I stopped in my tracks to look over.

Two men stood next to what appeared to be a tripod and a video camera. They saw me looking straight at them, but they never acknowledged my awareness of their presence. No movement. No words were spoken.

I shrugged it off, proceeded to my car, and drove away.

All weekend I fumed over the time and expectations that I had wasted with the colonel and his scheme to defraud the government and at the same time steal my money. On Monday morning I went to work at Topps.

A call came in. I answered it.

"Errol Steven Sachs?" the caller said.

"Yes," I said. "You're speaking to him."

He read the first part of my Social Security number and

asked me to verify the last four digits.

I did so and asked, "Who is this?"

"This is agent Nolan from FBI headquarters in New York City. We want to talk to you."

"About what?"

"We have Colonel Miller in custody, and we are expecting your statement on your possible involvement in an illegal matter pertaining to a position in an Army training program."

My involvement in an illegal matter? I didn't do anything wrong.

I took down the agent's contact information and immediately called my cousin Martin for some legal advice.

"I'm not a criminal lawyer, Stevie," he said, "but I'm going to refer you to a very good one. He's a disabled man—a paraplegic—and he has a brilliant legal mind. He will take very good care of you."

I made the call, and within an hour I was in the office of Attorney Michael Swanton. He met me at the door to his office, and using his crutches, swung his legs forward and made his way back to a seat behind his desk. The desk was strewn with papers so haphazardly scattered that the surface of the desk was totally obscured.

How could he ever find anything there?

His clothes were disheveled, and he had a long, unkempt beard that draped down over his chest. Since he was only about five feet, one inch tall, his long beard made him appear even shorter.

I began to have doubts that my cousin had made the proper referral.

Swanton wasted no time in collecting the details of my story. Then he asked for the contact information of the FBI agent who called me. He dialed the number. He spoke clearly and decisively to the agent who answered. "Mr. Nolan, I am sitting in my office with my client, Mr. Errol Steven Sachs. I want you to know that there is no fucking way Mr. Sachs is going to testify in the case involving Colonel Miller. Mr. Sachs did nothing wrong and he is an innocent victim in this matter."

I watched as Swanton listened to the agent's response, and then Swanton's voice exploded into the telephone receiver. "I don't give a fuck that you have him on tape and that you have videos of him walking into and out of the colonel's home. You did not have his permission to allow an audio recording of his conversations, and if you do have these recordings, then you obviously know that he refused to accept the appointment to the six-month program, and furthermore, you know that the reason he refused to enlist in this program is that he became aware of the colonel's illegal scheme."

He listened again to the agent's reply and then he continued with his adamant, inflexible position. "Mr. Nolan, I want this to be perfectly clear. My client will not say a fuckin' word to you and will not testify in this matter. You have to come up with something better if you want him to talk. In the meantime, go fuck yourself." He slammed the phone down on the receiver.

Then he looked over at me with a sly smile. "We'll probably hear back from them in a few days," he said.

I no longer had any misgivings. I knew that I had the right lawyer.

CHAPTER 7

The FBI, the CIA, and Me

MY ENTANGLEMENT WITH the colonel and the potential charges against me related to the Army recruitment saga just wouldn't go away.

One day while I was at Topps, I received a phone call. It was my lawyer, Mr. Swanton.

"Stevie," he said. "I need you to come down to my office the day after tomorrow. I've had another conversation with the FBI. This time it was a bit more cordial. I think you should tell them your side of the story."

"I thought I was free and clear."

"Not quite. There are some technical issues here that they can pursue, so I think it's wise for us to put all of this to bed."

Two days later I met with two FBI agents in Swanton's office. I answered all their questions directly and honestly. They kept pressing me on the matter of the first cash payment to the colonel and the fact that I had willingly brought a second cash payment to his house. They also played the audio recordings of my conversations with the colonel. Although I had refused to give him the second payment and vociferously withdrew from that sham six-month program, they continued to claim that I was a willing participant in a crime. They offered a deal—a fine, probation but no prison time—if I would plead guilty.

I looked at Swanton.

He shook his head and then leaned forward in his chair. "No fuckin' way my client pleads guilty here. He's a victim in this case."

The FBI agents looked at each other and then they closed their leather folders, stood up, and left the office.

Two weeks went by.

Once again, I thought I was in the clear.

Another call came in from Swanton.

"Stevie, I need you to come down to my office."

"What for?" I asked.

"The FBI agents want to talk to you again."

"But I've already told them everything I know about that crooked colonel. Why are they hassling me? I didn't do anything wrong."

"They told me they have an offer that will allow them to drop all of the charges against you."

"What kind of an offer?"

"I don't know, but I think it's worth listening to what they have to say."

I hesitated for a few seconds. "All right. What time should I be there?"

"Ten o'clock. My office. Be on time."

"I'm always on time. Just don't let these guys try to trick me into more trouble than I already have."

"Don't worry. You've got me. I'll keep you out of trouble." He laughed and hung up his phone.

Two days later I arrived at his office promptly at ten a.m.

The two FBI agents that I had met previously were already seated in my lawyer's small conference room. This time they were joined by another man with a flat-top haircut, broad shoulders, solid frame, and with a mean-looking countenance. There was an intimidating presence about him.

I wondered if the guy ever smiled.

"Steve," the lead FBI agent said, "I'd like you to meet Rod."

Rod extended his hand toward me, and I grasped it firmly.

"Nice to meet you," I said.

Rod nodded slightly and said nothing. His face remained expressionless.

"Are you with the FBI?" I asked.

The first agent interrupted before Rod could answer. "Uh, no, Rod is with another branch of the government. We'll get to that later."

I glanced at my lawyer.

He held out his hand with a slight tapping gesture, indicating that I should settle down and not be too aggressive with a follow-up. I had the distinct feeling that my lawyer had met with these guys well before my arrival and that he had been convinced that the charges against me would not easily go away unless I cooperated. I was fuming inside but managed to corral my anger. I could feel my heart pounding with anticipation.

Is this a set-up?

I sat down in a chair next to my lawyer at the oval-shaped table.

Everyone seemed uneasy.

Had someone just sucked the air out of the room?

Finally the lead FBI agent broke the ice and opened the discussion. "Steve," he said, "I'll let Rod fill you in about why we've asked you to meet with us today."

Rod sat up stiffly in his chair and stared across at me. He had a weathered, ruddy complexion that made me think he made his bones in outdoor activities.

"As you know, Steve, the charges against you are very

serious. And you got involved with a corrupt recruiter who is definitely going to prison. But after reviewing the details of your situation with the FBI, we agree that you may be an innocent victim in this matter. If you cooperate with us, we can make these charges go away."

"You want me to testify against the colonel?"

"Not at all."

"Then what do I have to do?"

"I'm in charge of a division of Special Forces for the United States Army. I deal with secret missions pertaining to issues of national concern. If you volunteer to be trained for and partake in an upcoming mission, I promise that you will be completely exonerated of all charges pertaining to the colonel's corruption case."

"What do I have to do in this mission?"

"We can't tell you now. All of that will be explained at the end of your training period—about six weeks of intensive military training."

"Sounds dangerous."

"All military operations have inherent danger."

I nodded. I knew exactly what he meant. I would be putting my life on the line if I said "Yes." But I also knew I was facing a huge risk if I turned them down and took my chances in a trial in which the deck seemed stacked against me. I sat silently, mulling over the possibilities of the offer.

He said I "may" be an innocent victim, but a judge might not see it that way.

Rod recognized my indecision and provided more details. "Keep in mind you are not enlisting in the Army for a two-year stint. You will be part of a group of limited engagement private contractors. If this mission does not go forward, if it is canceled for any reason, your engagement is finished and our deal with you still stands. All charges against you will be dropped. Your slate will be wiped clean."

I looked over to my lawyer for some guidance.

He raised his eyebrows and nodded as he put his hand on my shoulder. "This is your best option, Steve. Take the deal."

I looked across at Rod and the two FBI agents. Their faces were blank—obviously not interested in offering any further details.

My mind was racing.

What am I getting into? This could be a dangerous mission— a life-altering experience, but there is no way I will submit to a guilty plea or a trial.

I sat up in my chair and gave them my answer. "I'm in."

CHAPTER 8

And Then There Was Cuba

TWO WEEKS LATER I boarded a plane at Marine Park Naval and Military Base in Queens, New York, and was flown to West Virginia. From the airport I was taken to a training facility in the Blue Mountain region. There I met three other young guys who, with me, comprised a four-man unit. We were told by our commander that there were other four-man units that would be deployed with us for our ultimate mission.

This mission would be outside of the United States.

Our training schedule was rigorous: daily sessions at the shooting range, white-water paddling, diving, swimming, ten-mile backpacking stints, and running in rough terrain.

The training was tough, but I loved it. I felt like I was in the best shape of my life.

All four of us in my unit bonded immediately and became a team in the truest sense of the word, each member totally responsible to the others. We were advised to keep our private lives totally separate and unknown to our other unit members. All of our thoughts should be focused on the team and the responsibilities that would come when our unknown mission was actually launched.

We knew intuitively that the survival of each individual

depended on a unit that was well trained and highly capable; therefore we pushed each other to the limit in all of our training exercises.

We took the advice of our commanding officer seriously and for the most part kept our private lives and personal backgrounds to ourselves. I had the distinct feeling that when our mission was finished, we would never see or talk to each other again.

Our unit of four consisted of Reese, Red Beard, Rafo, and me. Reese was very quiet, but a fiercely focused person, totally consumed with training and preparing his body for our unknown mission.

Red Beard was a unique individual, somewhat strange in his habits, such as humming all the while he was eating and in particular while he was shooting his rifle. He was also a marksman—hitting the most bullseyes at the shooting range of anyone in our unit. I was second best in this category and took pride in my ability to handle a gun.

One day at the range I asked him, "Do you always hum while you're shooting?"

He seemed taken aback, and then he shrugged and said, "Keeps me relaxed. Focused. Need to be focused when I'm squeezin' that trigger."

"Red Beard's your nickname. What's your real name?"

He looked away for a few seconds and then turned to look straight into my eyes—a near defiant stare. "No one here needs to know my name. When this fuckin' thing is over, I'm just gonna vanish. Put this behind me."

I just nodded and said nothing, feeling that it was best not to pursue the conversation any further.

Rafo was the third guy. He appeared to be in his early twenties, definitely of Latin descent, because of his strong accent. He was a passionate guy, dependable, physically strong, and dedicated. Some of our training exercises involved challenges in which we had to rescue one of our unit members. Rafo and I always teamed up together. I trusted him to come through for me always.

One day, after a particularly tough training session, we sat on the grass drinking from our water jugs and trying to catch our breath. He asked me, "Why are you here?"

The off-limits nature of his question surprised me, but I decided to answer it anyway. "I got into some trouble with a crooked Army recruiter. This was my way out."

He nodded in a knowing manner but didn't give a response.

We sat quietly for a few seconds. An awkward silence.

"What about you?" I asked.

He looked down, aimlessly tossing a few blades of grass into the air and letting the breeze carry them away. Then he looked back at me. "For me, it's personal," he said.

"Personal?"

"Yes. I'm Cuban."

I asked nothing more.

From that moment I had a feeling that our secret mission would take us to Cuba.

After six weeks of intense training, our unit was taken to a facility known as The Bunker, on the grounds of The Greenbriar Resort in West Virginia. We entered through a large steel door built into the side of a hill. We walked through the facility with a uniformed soldier who provided a guided tour and discussion of the historical significance of the bunker. It was designed and built in 1957 as a haven for members of Congress in the event of a nuclear attack on the United States. I sensed that the message of the tour was to further instill a sense of patriotism in the mission we were about to undertake.

In the late afternoon two days later, we boarded a mid-sized submarine in Miami with seven other four-man units.

As we were boarding, I turned to Red Beard. "Whaddya think?" I asked.

He sneered. "About what?"

"You have an idea where we're headed?"

"Doesn't matter," he said. "Just someplace where we might get our asses blown off."

After we finished boarding, we were assembled to be informed of our final destination. It came as no surprise when the commanding officer said, "Gentlemen, we're on our way to Cuba."

Thinking back to the meeting with Rod in my lawyer's office, this entire operation had CIA written all over it.

During the one-and-a-half-hour trip from Miami, we were briefed on the details of our secret mission. The submarine would take us near the shores of a river—the Rio de Oro—that flowed into Cuba. We would stay on the submerged submarine until darkness. Under the cover of dark, the sub would surface and we would debark onto eight large raft boats that would each hold one four-man unit as well as the munitions and supplies we were delivering.

Our mission was to bury the weapons and boxes of ammunition on the riverbed so they could be used by the rebel forces seeking to overthrow Fidel Castro's oppressive government.

All of us listened intently.

I looked around the room. Many of the unit members were Hispanic. My guess: Cuban expatriates who, like Rafo, were supporters of the rebellion.

Everyone appeared calm. There were no nervous glances, whispers, or gestures. No comments were made. No questions were asked. Everyone seemed to understand the purpose and risks of our mission.

Our submarine arrived at the mouth of the Rio de Oro at nine p.m. After it surfaced, one by one, each unit inflated its assigned large raft boat, slipped it into the water, and loaded a large supply of rectangular boxes that contained rifles and ammunition. The boxes were sealed in plastic wrap to prevent water damage to the contents. Each unit was also given four trenching shovels designed for digging in sand.

Once all of the rafts were loaded, we followed our commanding officer's raft boat in single file and paddled down the river. Within forty-five minutes he signaled for us to follow him in turning ashore. After landing we dragged our rafts across a small sandy beach and hid them in a thickly wooded area behind the beach.

We unloaded our supplies and began digging. We dug trenches four feet deep, six feet long throughout the night, with the objective of burying at least half our supply of rectangular boxes into the trenches.

After a while I stopped for a minute to wipe the sweat off my face. I looked over to Rafo and whispered, "At least we have the moonlight to see what we're doing."

"Yes," he said.

"I feel like a gravedigger."

Rafo smiled. "A grave is for a dead man. This trench and the weapons we put in it will give my people a chance for a new life, a life of freedom."

I leaned toward him. "Rafo, you're an American citizen. You're free. Are you coming back here to join this fight? Looks like it could be very dangerous."

He stopped digging and stuck his shovel into the sand. "Let me ask you," he said, "would you fight for your family?"

"Yes, of course. With everything I had. There'd be no stopping me."

He smiled. "Then you already know my answer."

I just nodded. His intentions were clear. Nothing I could say would have changed his mind. We both picked up our shovels and continued digging.

After a few minutes he looked over to me. "Maybe someday you come back to visit me? We'll sit on this beach for some rum and a cigar."

We both then smiled widely.

"You've got a deal, my friend," I said.

Just before dawn we received a signal to stop working and retreat to the wooded area, where we hid and rested all through the day. It was a desolate area.

We were ordered to keep conversation to a minimum and make no loud noises that would draw attention to our presence in the area; thus there was hardly any talking and definitely no boisterous laughter whatsoever. Most guys slept and kept to themselves. Each unit of four spread out at the edge of the wooded area and provided guard duty for one hour at a time.

The only noises were the sounds of nature: birds chirping, bugs and mosquitoes buzzing.

During this time, we saw no one.

At night we resumed our digging operation and finished burying the remaining supply of boxes. The commanding officer and his crew took a series of precise measurements using subtlety marked trees at the edge of the wooded area as landmarks. We assumed the measurements would be provided to the rebels to help them recover the stash of buried weapons and ammunition.

We packed up our gear and began pulling our raft boats toward the river and our ultimate rendezvous with the submarine. Just as we got to the edge of the river, a series of gunshots rang out. We had no idea where the gunfire was coming from or who was doing the shooting.

We were on an open beach with nowhere to hide.

"Stay low, get on your rafts, and get the hell out of here," our commanding officer yelled.

Some guys screamed in pain, hit by the sudden barrage of bullets. It became a scene of complete chaos. My unit clambered to push our boat farther out on the river, and then, one by one, we climbed into our boat.

Reese, Red Beard, me, and then Rafo.

Reese and Red Beard began paddling furiously while I reached back to help Rafo climb aboard. He appeared to be weak and unable to pull himself up on his own. I grabbed him under his arms and pulled him up and over the edge of the raft. His body was limp, so I rolled him over to see if he had been hit.

I was shocked at what I saw. His shirt was covered with blood.

He struggled to talk, but no sounds came out of his mouth. In an instant I knew why. Rafo had a large, gaping hole in his neck, his throat nearly shattered. I pulled up my shirt and used it as a cloth in a desperate attempt to stop the bleeding. "Rafo! Rafo! Hang in there, man!" I yelled.

But it was no use. There was nothing I could do. Within seconds he was dead.

Reese and Red Beard kept paddling but turned to look back at me when they heard the commotion. They both bore anxious, painful looks.

"Rafo?" asked Reese.

I swallowed hard, almost unable to get the words out. My eyes welled up. "He's gone," I said.

Reese and Red Beard looked dazed. They turned and resumed paddling as we moved farther away from trouble.

I held Rafo in my arms until we arrived at the submarine. The whole time I thought of missed opportunities, the days I could have devoted even more time talking to him, finding out more details about his passion for the mission. I could have learned about his family. Did he have a wife, a girlfriend, parents, brothers and sisters in Cuba? Is that why he was willing to risk his life to overthrow Castro? I could have been his friend, perhaps developed a lifetime friendship. Instead I sat in a rubber raft holding his dead body.

The crew of the submarine helped to remove Rafo's body and placed it in a holding area until we returned to Miami.

Once we got off the submarine, we were debriefed and underwent a complete physical examination by a medical team.

The officers and doctors were cold and matter-of-fact in all of their words and actions. Not one of them expressed sympathy or even a hint of compassion about our losses or the stress and mental trauma we might have suffered in the covert operation. The debriefing was a joke. I was simply advised not to discuss the mission with anyone, especially the press.

Two days later I was on an Amtrak train from Miami to New York.

The newspapers had headlines about the failed rebellion to overthrow Castro's government at the Bay of Pigs and editorials that focused on the foreign policy embarrassment to President Kennedy's young administration.

I didn't read them. Instead I sat alone on the train, looking out the window and pondering the events of the past few weeks.

So many young men were sacrificed because of a bungled CIA operation.

As expected, I never heard from Reese or Red Beard.

In fact, I never even said goodbye to either one of them

CHAPTER 9

Frank DeAngelis and a Loaf of Bread

MY LATE TEENS and early twenties can be best described as the years when I bounced around.

After graduating from high school, I started my college education at Philadelphia Textile Institute (PTI)—ultimately a college of many names—located in the East Falls section of Philadelphia. In 1961 the school changed its name to the Philadelphia College of Textiles and Science, and then in 1999 to simply Philadelphia University. Finally in 2017 the school merged with Jefferson Medical College and to form Thomas Jefferson University, dropping its original name altogether.

PTI primarily prepared students to be fashion engineers and designers, so I stayed there for only one year and eventually transferred to NYU. It's a good thing I did: I could not imagine myself as part of the fashion industry. Besides, if I told people I was a graduate of PTI, they wouldn't know what the hell I was talking about.

During all my college years I worked part-time for my father.

My parents were separated at that time, and my mom still worked as a bookkeeper. When I was not working with my father in the meat plant, I was out selling, trying to find new customers and expand the business.

One of our customers was Spiro's Coffee Shop, operated by a guy named Vinny who happened to be not only a customer, but also a good friend of my father's. Vinny was a pleasant guy, but I had always heard that he liked to cut corners to save a few bucks. Vinny was also a compulsive gambler and owed big money to the bookies. When you owed money to the bookies in New York, by extension you owed money to the Mob, and when the debt got high enough, the Mob controlled you.

However, one of Vinny's biggest debts was to the federal government. He had not paid any federal income tax in three years.

One day at seven a.m. the phone rang in our meat plant.

"Hello," the man said. "Can I speak to Ben?"

"Sorry," I said. "He's out right now. This is his son, Steve. Can I help you?"

"Your father's friend, Vinny, has a big problem. There are three federal agents standing outside his door with a padlock and chains. They're gonna shut down his restaurant unless he pays his overdue taxes."

"But how can my father help with that?"

"Vinny needs seven thousand dollars in cash."

"Who are you?"

"I'm Frank DeAngelis, the president of the Restaurant Workers Union... local number one hundred. Vinny called me over here to help him out of this mess. Vinny says your father always keeps cash in the safe at his shop."

I knew he was right. My father always had cash stored in the safe. He loved cash deals so he could hide money from the government. Like his friend Vinny, my father tried to avoid paying income tax in any way possible. However, I was not about to hand over seven thousand dollars without my father's approval, and there was no way for me to reach him for at least a few hours.

"Sorry, Mr. DeAngelis, I can't give you seven thousand dollars without my father's say so."

A long pause. I wondered if he had hung up on me.

Then he spoke in very measured, but direct tones. "Listen, kid. We have an important connection here. Vinny is a very good customer of your father's. If he gets shut down, it's gonna hurt your father's business in a big way. Your father is not gonna be happy about that. And he is not gonna be happy with you for not listening to me. So go to the safe and get the seven thousand, and then get your ass over here right away." His voice rose by the end of the sentence.

It was a powerful message. Yes, even more of a threat.

"All right," I said. "I'll be there in twenty minutes."

I went to the safe and took out $7,000 in hundred-dollar bills. I stuffed the money into a cloth baseball bag that I kept with my gear, hopped into the van, and drove over to Spiro's Coffee Shop, located on 7th Avenue and 12th Street near St. Vincent's Hospital. Spiro's proximity to the hospital provided a steady stream of customers all day and night. As a result, Spiro's stayed open 24/7 and proved to be a cash cow for Vinny.

The traffic was light, so I was able to arrive on time.

I walked into the office. I was breathing heavily from a combination of the rush to get there and the uncertainty and anxiety of handing so much money to a total stranger.

Vinny sat at his desk next to a handsome man who had taken the center chair behind the desk. The man had a dark complexion, black hair with some strands of gray, and was dressed in a black suit with a black shirt. The man appeared to be about fifty years old. He looked up at me and smiled. "I'm

Frank DeAngelis," he said as he stood and reached out to shake my hand.

"Nice to meet you," I said, shaking his hand and trying to gather my composure.

"You made a good decision here, kid … a very nice job. Tell your father we'll pay it back in two days."

I nodded. "Here you go," I said as I put the baseball bag down on the desk and slid it over to him.

Frank didn't bother to look inside the bag or count the money. Instead, he invited me to sit down, have some breakfast, and talk to him for a while. It was nothing more than polite conversation, the usual stuff: where I grew up, where I was going to school, my softball career, and what kind of work I did for my father. But there was certain warmth about the guy that was disarming.

I began to relax and sensed that he liked me for listening to him and following through with the delivery.

Within half an hour, I was back in the van on my way back to the meat store.

I found out months later that the seven thousand dollars was used to pay off the feds who were waiting outside—a cash bribe. Spiro's was never closed, not even for a minute, and Vinny's tax liability to the federal government miraculously vanished. This was a form of justice that only the Mob could obtain.

When my father came back to the store and heard what I had done, he exploded with anger. "You went into the safe and took seven thousand dollars?" he yelled.

"Mr. DeAngelis said it was important for the business. He said you would definitely do the same thing yourself," I said.

"Do you know who fuckin' Frank DeAngelis is?"

"He said he was the president of a restaurant workers' union," I said with an apologetic tone.

My father let out a sarcastic laugh. "He's also a big shot in the Mob, for Chrissakes! You handed seven grand over to the Mob."

"But he said he'd pay you back."

My father waved me off. He was clearly pissed off at me. There was no use trying to reason with my father when it came to money. He was cheap and could never step back to see the big picture.

The next day Frank DeAngelis called again. My father answered the phone. His eyes widened when he realized who was on the other end of the call.

"Hey, Frank, what's this I hear about the seven grand my son gave you yesterday?" His voice had a definite edge of annoyance.

I couldn't hear Frank's response, but I guessed he was reassuring my father that the money would be paid back in two days as promised.

"And what's the vig on this loan?" my father asked.

I watched intently as he listened to Frank's response, and then he erupted in anger. "No vig? Whaddya' mean, no vig?" He listened again for about a minute and then spoke in a much more conciliatory tone. "All right, all right, I get it, Frank. It's good for business. Just get the money back to me, and we'll be square."

I picked up on something in the exchange: there was an apologetic element in my father's voice during his last response. The outrage and bluster he had directed toward me the day before had suddenly vanished. I had the distinct feeling that he was afraid of Frank DeAngelis.

But their conversation was not over.

"You want to speak to my son?" my father asked. My father looked bewildered as he listened to Frank's reply. "Okay, I'll send him over," he said as he hung up. My father had a confused look on his face. "Frank DeAngelis wants to see you over at Spiro's." He paused for a few seconds, apparently trying to process his own words. He looked over to me quizzically. "Why would he want to talk to you?"

"I have no idea."

"Well, you better get your ass over there right now."

I grabbed the keys to the van, put on my jacket, and hustled out the door. For the second time in just two days, I had been ordered to get my ass over to Spiro's.

The traffic was very light. I got there in fifteen minutes and parked the van in the alleyway in the rear of the coffee shop. I walked inside and looked around. Frank DeAngelis sat in a booth and waved me over. As I had noticed the day before, he was dressed impeccably, that day in gray and black.

"Sit down, Stevie," he said. "Order some breakfast. It's on me."

"Thanks," I said, still wondering why this guy wanted to talk to me.

Had I miscounted the money yesterday? Was something wrong?

The waitress brought over a cup of coffee, and I ordered scrambled eggs and a side of bacon.

When she walked away, Frank leaned over the table to talk more privately. "I did some checking up on you, kid," he said.

"On me?"

"Yeah. You grew up in Brooklyn...the Asshole End, right?"

I laughed. "That's what some people called it," I said.

"I know some young guys that remember you from that area. They say you were a pretty tough kid. Got into some rough scrapes with them."

"Which guys?"

He shrugged. "A few of the Gambino boys, Tommy F., a few others."

"Yeah, we had our share of street fights. Haven't seen those guys in a while. I've been busy with school and working with my father. Are they doing okay?"

"Oh yeah, they're doing just fine. They're ..." He caught himself mid-sentence and hesitated for a few seconds.

I sensed that he was not interested in providing any more details. I had heard rumors about my former friends, that they were involved in some heavy-duty illegal activities. But I decided that this was not the time to pursue that topic with Frank DeAngelis. I just let it go and waited for him to make the next statement.

He moved a little closer and leaned farther over the table toward me. "You and your Dad have a nice little business going there."

"Yes," I said. "Things are going pretty well, but we're trying to grow it even bigger."

He laughed a little and then held his hands out toward me, a few inches apart. "Son, what you have now is a very small loaf of bread." He spread his hands apart, almost a foot wide. "If you and your father work your asses off seven days a week, you may be able to get that loaf of bread to be this big."

He then moved his hands farther apart, about a yard wide. "But with my help, you can have a loaf this big," he said.

He smiled widely, obviously impressed with his own narrative, and then paused to take a sip from his coffee. He then leaned across the table even closer to me and spoke in a near whisper. "I can get accounts for you that will be required to buy your meat. They will have no choice. These stores buy where I tell them to buy. Your business will grow four maybe five times bigger in less than a year."

I was nearly speechless at the prospects of such success. "Thank you," I blurted out. "That would be terrific."

He sat back a little and eyed me carefully. "Kid, you are very well thought of. You've got a good reputation around Brooklyn and here. You know how to take care of yourself, and you're a hard worker. I was very impressed with the way you handled that situation yesterday. A lot of young people would have been scared shitless to do what you did—go into their father's safe, take out seven K and give it to a guy they never met. But you had balls. Big balls. You figured out that it was important for business, and you took care of business."

I was humbled by the compliment and again, almost speechless, but I managed to utter a quick "Thank you" before taking another gulp of coffee.

Frank DeAngelis wasn't finished making his point. He held his hands wide apart, demonstrating again his image of the large loaf of bread. "This large loaf of bread can happen only with my help." He lowered his hands as if carefully placing the large loaf on the table in front of us, and then, with a dramatic flair, he slammed his right hand down like a knife chopping the loaf in half. "Then this will be my half and this will be your half. If you team up with me, your business gets bigger beyond your imagination. But half of it will belong to me."

The sound of his hand slamming down on the table startled some of the other diners in the coffee shop. They looked over at us to see what was going on. Several people stared for a few seconds.

Frank DeAngelis stared back with a fearsome, menacing look. Evidently this was his way of telling onlookers to stay out of his private conversations.

It worked. Gradually everyone looked away.

"I appreciate the offer, Frank," I said. "But I have to talk this over with my father and think about it for a few days."

He threw his hands up in a conciliatory gesture. "Of course, of course! No problem. How 'bout we get together in a week or so? I'll call you to set up a date."

We finished eating breakfast, and I got up from the table.

As I was about to leave, he reached into his pocket and pulled out a business-size envelope that appeared to be stuffed with paper, almost bursting at the seams. "Oh," he said. "Give this to your father."

I lifted the open flap of the envelope and quickly glanced at the contents. It contained a thick stack of one-hundred-dollar bills.

When I got to my van, I counted the money. The envelope contained seven thousand dollars.

I drove back to the store and handed the envelope to my father. "This is from Frank DeAngelis. It's a day early."

My father opened the envelope, counted the money, and then walked back to the safe and put the envelope inside.

I resumed trimming briskets in the back of the shop.

My father came over to me. He had a troubled look on his face. "What did he want?" he asked.

"He just wanted to return your money."

My father looked at me, seemingly still trying to figure out what was happening, but said nothing, and then he walked away.

I never said a word about the offer from Frank DeAngelis.

While I was making deliveries during the next few days, I made it a point to learn more about Frank DeAngelis from several of our customers who owned restaurants and other small diners. They were people with whom I had established a trustworthy relationship. I knew I could speak to them in confidence.

Dmitri Soulos owned a small coffee shop and diner on East Side. Dmitri was a happy, good-natured guy who always had a smile on his face. I placed the box with his order of brisket on the countertop in the kitchen. "Dmitri, I've got a question for you," I said.

"What makes you think I have an answer?" he said with a laugh.

"I met a guy, Frank DeAngelis. What do you know about him?"

Dmitri's smile vanished instantly, and his mouth dropped slightly open. He paused, eyeing me carefully for a few seconds. "Frank? Frank DeAngelis? You want to know about him?"

"Yes."

As if governed by fear of reprisal, Dmitri looked around to make sure no one else could hear our conversation. When he spoke, his voice was very low—almost a whisper. "Frank's the president of Local number one hundred," he said, "but he's much more than that. He's a big deal with the Mob...high up in the ranks. He rules the union workers in the restaurant business with an iron hand...controls everybody, including us owners. Diners, restaurants, even sandwich shops. You don't cross him by hiring a nonunion worker. If you do, you get a visit from Frank or one of his guys."

"He roughs you up?"

He shrugged, and then with a slight twinkle in his eye said, "Not really. Usually it's a 'conversation,' but you get the message. Things get more serious if you don't pay your brokerage fee."

"Brokerage fee?"

"Oh, yeah. Frank gets a cut on our supply orders. All our paper products come through a company recommended by Frank. We get a discount off the retail price and then pay Frank the brokerage in cash."

The owners with whom I spoke gave me a similar story. They respected Frank DeAngelis, but they also feared him. Everyone knew that Frank was in charge and that he had plenty of muscle in the Mob to back him up.

Five days later I met Frank DeAngelis at Spiro's Coffee Shop for the third time. He sat in a booth with a middle-aged man. Frank stood up and said, "Hey, Stevie, meet Jimmy Blue Eyes. He owns a few restaurants on the East Side of Manhattan."

Jimmy stood up to shake my hand. He was small-statured, about five feet six inches, with a large bald spot that looked like it would soon meet up with his forehead.

"If you ever need a loan," Frank said, "Jimmy's the guy who can help you out."

I took that statement to mean that Jimmy Blue Eyes was a loan shark.

We all sat down in the booth.

Frank started the conversation. "Well, what did your father have to say about my offer?"

"I never discussed it with him."

He looked surprised. "But it's his business, right?"

"Yes, but some day I'm gonna own it. And when that day comes, I don't want to share my loaf of bread with anyone else. I hope there are no hard feelings, Mr. DeAngelis, but I have to turn down your offer."

Frank stared at me for a few seconds, seemingly taken aback by my comments.

I had the immediate feeling that he was not used to having one of his offers rejected.

Then he flashed a wide smile. He reached over and lightly slapped me on the cheek. "Good for you, kid. Good for you."

"No disrespect, sir. You're a gentleman and I appreciate your offer, but I want to run my business my way, and I want to build it myself."

He gave out a friendly laugh and held his arms out wide.

"Hey, this is America. You gotta respect a kid who wants to work hard and become successful." He laughed harder and looked over to Jimmy Blue Eyes for reassurance.

Jimmy nodded. "Right on, Frankie, right on."

"Listen, kid," Frank continued. "If you ever need anything, don't be afraid to call me. Go on your own way in life, but feel free to hang out with us anytime our paths cross."

Our brief meeting was over. We shook hands.

I left Spiro's Coffee Shop.

That was the beginning of my long and beneficial relationship with Frank DeAngelis. He never interfered with my business. Rather, he introduced me to people who eventually helped my business.

Years later, through him, I met Charlie Anselmo, who was not only an important person in the Bonnano family but who also became an important person in my life.

CHAPTER 10

The Probation Cop

IN 1970 THE Cuba situation was in my rearview mirror, and I had to move on and make a living. I wasn't on particularly great terms with my father, so I began looking for a job. My uncle contacted me and offered me a job in construction on Long Island. At the time, he owned a large tract of land and had a contract to build more than 250 houses in a three-year period in several Long Island communities—Setauket, Center Reach, and Lake Grove, among others, so I went to work for him as a construction supervisor.

I moved into an apartment with a friend of my cousin. My roommate, however, spent all of his nights at his girlfriend's place, so I pretty much had the apartment to myself. This arrangement suited me just fine.

I decided to host a party one Saturday night and invited a large group of friends to attend. It was a great party—lots of great food, beer and wine—and lasted into the wee hours of the morning.

I was still very active in the Brooklyn Softball League and had a playoff game against Lincoln Terrace on Sunday morning. After all the partying, I struggled to wake up. In fact, when I opened one eye at 5:30 a.m. and looked at my alarm clock, I realized that I had slept right through the alarm and was going to be late for the game. I jumped out of bed, took a fast shower, and put on my uniform shirt. I stepped over the guys and gals sleeping on the floor as I quietly made my way out of the apartment to my Austin Healy parked on the street.

Within minutes I was on the Interboro Parkway headed into Brooklyn. Traffic was light, and despite the many curves on the roadway, I sped along at a high speed, darting in and out between cars, trying to make up the time I lost by oversleeping. In the process I inadvertently cut off another car.

The driver was pissed and blasted his horn at me. But it was New York, where most drivers had one hand on the wheel and the other on the horn, so I ignored him and kept driving. Next thing I knew, his car pulled up in the lane next to me.

The guy's face was red with anger, and he shook his fist toward me. He flipped his middle finger as he sped about a car length ahead. Without signaling, he suddenly swerved into my lane, cutting me off, and missing my front bumper by inches. He no sooner got in front of me than he stepped on his brakes, forcing me to slam on mine to avoid a rear-end collision. As I screeched to a near stop, he floored it, accelerating his car ahead to Pennsylvania Avenue.

I pulled alongside of him and made a gesture of apology, but he was having none of it and continued his angry rant.

I shrugged, drove ahead, and made a left turn onto Pennsylvania Avenue. After a five-minute ride I made a right turn onto a side street just before Linden Boulevard. As I approached a stop sign, he suddenly pulled in front of my car and blocked it from going forward. He got out of his car and came toward me.

He was wearing a beige shirt typical of young probation cops who were in their final six months of training before becoming full-time New York police officers.

I got out of my car.

As he stormed toward me, I could see the rage in his face, and I could also see that he was holding a billy club in his left hand. Without warning he swung it wildly at me and grazed my right eyebrow. Blood splattered onto my face and flowed into my right eye, clouding my vision. Instinctively I leaned over and landed a solid right-handed punch to his groin.

He went down in a heap.

Still stunned by the blow to my head, I tried to clear my vision with the shirtsleeve of my softball uniform. When I looked back, he was hobbling down the street behind a group of Orthodox Jews on their way to Sunday prayers.

My head was throbbing, but I chased after him and caught him in front of a row of brownstone houses.

He continued to clutch his billy club, so I knew he was still dangerous. I turned him around and hit him with a left and a right.

The cut above my eye was bleeding profusely, and I had to stop for a few seconds to wipe my eye and once again clear my vision.

In the meantime, he crawled away toward a house with a metal fence in the front. As he looked back at me, he tossed his billy club onto the roof of a one-story garage and then limped into the front courtyard of the house.

I caught up to him, grabbed him by his hair, and pulled him down to the ground on his back. He let out a painful groan, but I didn't care. The guy had cracked my head open with a billy club, and I was determined to make him pay.

As he lay on his back, I slammed the gate of the fence back and forth on his head a few times. He tried to get away, but his energy was totally spent.

His adrenaline suddenly kicked in. He pulled up on all fours and lunged forward toward a garbage can. He picked up the cover and used it as a shield to protect his head from any further blows.

I took off my garrison belt and kept banging away at the garbage can cover as he cowered below it and remained curled up on the ground. He cried out in pain and begged me to stop.

A small crowd gathered, and people began yelling and screaming. Before I knew it, the street was full of cops. I knew I was in trouble.

The probation cop crawled up on his knees and then slowly got to his feet. As he gathered himself and took a deep breath, he pointed to me. "I'm a probation officer, and this man attacked me," he yelled.

Two police officers rushed over and held him up by the arms as they assisted him to a seat in a police cruiser.

An older officer wearing a badge that read "Sergeant" approached me. He looked at the gash in my eyebrow and called back to one of the younger men. "Bring a towel over here so this guy can stop his bleeding."

Within seconds the young officer handed a white towel to me.

"Thanks," I said as I pressed the towel against my eyebrow to stop the flow of blood.

The sergeant stared at me, seemingly trying to size up the situation. "What happened here?" he barked.

"Your probation cop had a severe case of road rage on the Interboro and came after me with a billy club when I tried to make a turn at a stop sign. This cut on my eye came from that billy club. I had no choice but to defend myself."

The sergeant looked around and then stared back at me. "I don't see any billy club lying around here," he said.

"He threw it up onto a garage roof."

"Which roof?" he asked with a heavy dose of skepticism. He put his hands on his hips and continued to focus on me with an angry glare.

I pointed to the garage. "Right there," I said.

The probation cop sat on the side of the back seat of the police cruiser and heard the conversation. "He's a lyin' bastard!" he yelled. "He cut me off on the highway and then attacked me when I pulled him over. I never hit him with a billy club."

An elderly woman walked over to the sergeant. "I live in that house right over there," she said as she pointed to a brownstone across the street. "I saw the whole thing."

"What did you see, ma'am," said the sergeant.

"I saw that man sitting in your police car come limping down the street, and this man standing next to you had blood running down on his face as he was chasing him. The man in your police car had some kind of a club in his hand. Then he threw it on the roof of that garage."

The sergeant motioned to one of his men. "Check out that roof to see if there's a billy club up there." He turned his attention back to the elderly woman. "Thank you, ma'am; we appreciate your help."

The elderly woman ambled away.

A few minutes later a young cop came over to the sergeant. He was holding the billy club. "Found this, sir," he said as he pointed to the roof of the garage.

The sergeant glared over at the probation cop but said nothing.

Another officer walked up to the sergeant and whispered in his ear. Both men looked over at the probation cop. The sergeant nodded, acknowledging the information that had just been imparted to him. He turned to the young cop as he pointed to me.

"Take this man to the Brookdale Hospital Emergency Room. That eye is going to need some stitches."

"What about the probation officer in the cruiser? Should I take him to the hospital too?" he asked.

"Not yet," the sergeant said. "I need to talk to him first."

I got into one of the police cars and was taken to the hospital. I needed five stitches and a bandage but passed all the concussion tests. As I was ready to leave the hospital, the nurse informed me that two people needed to talk to me in one of the consultation rooms. She escorted me to a small room off to the side of the registration area.

Two men sat at a small table. One of the men wore a police uniform with a badge that read "Captain." The other man wore a black suit, a white shirt, and a black tie.

Was he a plainclothes cop or an undertaker?

The captain spoke first. "Take a seat, Steve. We need to talk for a minute."

I sat down in a chair facing the two men.

"Steve, I'm Captain O'Neil, and this is Jim McDonnell, our department administrator. You know that you were engaged in an altercation with a probation trainee who is soon to become a New York City police officer?"

"Yeah, I've seen some of those guys around. I could tell by his beige-colored shirt."

"And you beat up this trainee pretty badly, including punching him in the face and slamming his head against a metal gate?"

"That's right, but he attacked me first with a billy club and busted open my forehead. He had no cause to do that."

The captain paused and looked over at McDonnell. McDonnell leaned over and whispered something into the captain's ear.

The captain nodded, looked back at me, and continued.

"Steve, we'd like to make this whole issue go away with no charges against you, provided that you lodge no charges against the probation trainee."

I hesitated for a few seconds. The fix was in, and I knew it. "So," I said, "you need to protect this guy so he can get on the police force without anything on his record, such as attacking a citizen with a billy club during a road-rage incident?"

Both men stared at me without answering.

Then the captain spoke. "Well, if you agree not to file charges, at least you'll have the satisfaction of knowing that you beat the shit out of the stupid asshole."

We all laughed.

"What do you say, Steve? We have a deal here? Case closed?" he asked.

"Sure," I said. "I get it. You guys have to sweep this incident away. But how do I get to my softball game? I'm late already."

The captain smiled. "Come with me. You're gonna have a police escort."

I hopped into a police cruiser.

The captain got behind the wheel. The blue lights began flashing as we whizzed by cars on Pennsylvania Avenue. He dropped me off at my car, and I arrived at the game in the beginning of the fifth inning.

We won.

CHAPTER 11

Hot Stuff

I CONTINUED WORKING as a construction supervisor for my uncle. In those days I was very fit—a muscular frame with very little or no body fat. I didn't have much of a wardrobe, so I went to work in a tight shirt and shorts.

The women who moved into these areas seemed to be on the prowl. On plenty of occasions some of them stopped by the construction trailer to strike up a conversation and ask about one of the new homes we were building. Some of these women seemed to have time on their hands. I tried to be friendly and polite, assuming that they could be a new buyer for one of the homes we were putting up. I also assumed their husbands went off to work in the mornings to earn enough money to pay for their new house.

One morning a woman sauntered into the construction trailer where I was doing some paperwork. She was wearing a bright red raincoat, which I found surprising, not because of its color, but because it wasn't raining. When she opened up the raincoat, there was nothing underneath it. She was totally naked. She invited me to her house.

I was twenty-nine. Of course I didn't refuse.

My uncle's partner, Angelo, had a son, Carl, who worked

with me. He was a bit of a whack job. His father had fired him twice, but I thought he deserved another chance, so I brought him back and put him to work alongside of me.

One day the crew was digging a hole for a concrete wall in Center Reach and Carl mouthed off to one of the workers. He thought he was a tough kid, and when I tried to intervene, he gave me a lot of shit.

Here I was, the guy who gave him a second chance, and he was talking smack to me?

"Who do you think you are, Mister Bigshot, always bossing me around?" he said.

I didn't say a thing, and I didn't waste any time. I took one swing and decked him.

He reeled backward and fell into a hole the crew was digging.

I knew he was stunned but not seriously injured, so I left him lying there and told the rest of the crew, "Keep an eye on this guy and make sure he keeps breathing." I walked back to the trailer.

My uncle looked up from his desk as I opened the door. The serious look on my face must have made him sense something was wrong. "What's up, Stevie?" he asked.

"I've been thinking that this job is not for me. I just had an incident with Angelo's son, Carl."

"What happened?"

"He got in my face, looking for a fight in front of the other workers."

My uncle rolled his eyes and tossed his pen on the desk in obvious frustration.

"Look," I said. "I don't want you to have trouble with your partner, so I'm leaving."

"You sure, Stevie?" he said.

"Yeah, I'm real sure. I'm outta here. It's best for all concerned."

My uncle didn't ask for the particulars, so I chose not to provide any. I had no doubt that he would get a full report from the rest of the workers. I never heard from the loudmouth in the ditch, but I'm sure some members of the crew hauled his ass out of there when he came to.

I bounced around for a couple of weeks, spent most of the money I had earned, and eventually took a job in Puerto Rico with a friend of mine.

Before I left, I contacted my father. Our relationship was always a challenge—up and down. I was never sure where it would go.

"Whaddya think about coming back to Topps and working with me again?" he asked.

"Maybe. But I just took a job down in Puerto Rico and don't want to back out of my commitment."

"I could really use you here. I'm thinking about expanding to a new plant over on 38th Street between 8th and 9th Avenue."

"Sounds good. Good luck with it."

He paused for a second, as he always did when he was struggling to find the right words. "Look," he said. "If you come back to work with me, I'll give you a partnership plan within a year or two. We can build a big business together." He seemed desperate, pleading with me to come back. It was an awkward moment.

"It's tempting," I said. "I'll have to think about it."

"How about if I give you the plans? You've been in construction. Look them over and tell me what you think. Okay?"

I agreed to review the plans and took them with me to Puerto Rico.

One day I sat on the beach reviewing the plans. My experience as a construction supervisor kicked in. I knew how to read and interpret the renovation plans. I also had some ideas about how to make improvements, the type that would create better efficiency of the entire operation as well as save money during the construction phase. The possibilities excited me.

Suddenly I was distracted by a beautiful babe standing in front of me. She was wearing a polka dot bikini that left little to the imagination.

"Why are you looking so intently at those papers instead of looking at me?" she asked.

May I remind you that I was twenty-nine?

"You have plans for tonight?" I asked.

"Just with you," she said.

"How about if I meet you at the casino at seven o'clock?"

She smiled. "It's a deal." She winked and walked away.

That was a walk that I still vividly recall to this day.

I got to the casino early and went to a craps table. Luck was with me. I was hot as a pistol. Within a short time I was up several hundred dollars. I kept making my number and letting it ride. When I looked down at my chips, I was up nearly a thousand.

Promptly at seven p.m., my "date" showed up, wearing a see-through dress.

She leaned over my shoulder and kissed me on the neck. "How are you doing, big guy?" she asked.

"Great, but even better now that you arrived." I promptly rolled a seven and lost a good portion of my winnings. I should have taken it as an omen of things to come.

We left the casino and went to a few nightclubs. The drinks flowed, and we were both feeling pretty good. She was a real hot dancer, and everybody seemed to stand back to watch her moves.

At one a.m. I took her back to my hotel room.

We were in bed in a highly passionate moment when suddenly she arched upward and began screaming, "Kill! Kill!"

I jumped out of bed in a near panic, assuming I had been set up. I turned on some lights and looked around. I made sure my wallet was still on the nightstand. I opened the closets, but no one was there, just the two of us.

She looked up at me with a curious smile. "You always do this when you're in the middle of fucking?"

I laughed and said, "You were screaming 'Kill, kill'. I thought you were setting me up."

It was her turn to laugh. "I was just trying to let you know you were killing it, man. Just killing it." She pulled down the sheet that was covering her body. "Come on back to bed," she said.

I didn't hesitate.

The rest of the night was sensational.

CHAPTER 12

Fast Pitch—Abrupt Ending

WHILE GROWING UP I enjoyed playing many different sports. My very favorite sport, however, was softball—not the slow-pitch variety, but fast-pitch softball. Once I had a chance to see Eddie Feigner—the founder and main attraction of the nationally known team King and His Court. I was hooked on the game and played it well into my forties.

King and His Court was a four-man team: pitcher, catcher, shortstop, and first baseman. Eddie Feigner, often described as "the greatest softball pitcher who ever lived," was truly a sight to behold. He had a forearm the size of a stovepipe and could throw a softball so fast that batters could hardly react before the ball exploded into the catcher's mitt. King and his Court toured all over the United States and various foreign countries, putting on exhibitions and challenging local teams to a game. They had an incredible record of success and entertained hundreds of thousands of fans.

In 1974 I was playing on several softball teams that played in and around New York. One of the teams was sponsored by McDonald's and competed in the Brooklyn Fast-Pitch League. It was a league comprised of many good players, mostly young working guys who found softball a great outlet for exercise, friendly competition, and of course, a little action.

Yes, action, meaning you showed up at the game with your softball glove and your wallet. Wagering on the outcome of these games was common and served as further incentive for the teams to play hard. The crowds weren't big, but even some of the folks who showed up to watch the game occasionally took part in the wagering. Why wouldn't they place a bet or two? After all, this was Brooklyn.

Our McDonald's team was solid. We had good hitters from top to bottom in our lineup and were always one of the top teams in the league. I was the oldest player on our team. I was also the only Jew.

Our main rival was always Shore Pride—another team loaded with talented players, one of whom was the first baseman and captain, Jack "Jackie" Cunningham. The history between the McDonald's team and the guys on Shore Pride was not only highly competitive; it was a bitter rivalry, downright nasty.

Jack Cunningham was connected to the Mob. Carlo Gambino was the godfather to Jackie's mother, and Jackie's businesses benefitted through this association. Unlike most members of the Mob that I knew, Jack flaunted his connections and made sure everyone knew about it. At times he hurled insults and invectives at his opponents, thinking that he was immune to retribution because of his inherent family protection. He never missed an opportunity to stir the pot, and in the process, proved to be an obnoxious jerk.

In one of our last games of the regular season, we were vying for the division title and hoping to move on to play for the championship. We were up against Cunningham's team that had similar designs to advance.

At the start of the game, as usual, the bet was $500 per team.

In the bottom of the seventh—the last inning—Shore Pride

was ahead four to two. Our team had two men on base with two out. Cunningham was at first base. As I walked up to the plate, Cunningham leaned in and yelled, "Hey, Jew boy, have any money left to bet?"

I stepped to the side of the batter's box. "Sure," I said. "How much you wanna put down?"

"A hundred says you strike out and we win the game."

I laughed. "Only a hundred? My two hundred says you don't get me out and we win the game."

Jack threw his arms up in disbelief. "No fuckin' way. I'll lay you five to two on that, pal. My five hundred to your two hundred."

The sparse crowd loved the confrontation.

"You're on, wise ass," I called out to him as I stepped back into the batter's box. I settled in, trying to focus on the pitcher who was known for a quick delivery motion and a great fast ball.

The pitcher threw his pitch—a high riser, right down the middle.

I swung hard and caught it square on the barrel.

Cunningham turned and watched as the ball sailed over the right field fence. A three-run homer.

In disgust he slammed his glove down on the ground.

We won the game five to four.

After our team celebration at home plate, I caught up with Cunningham near his bench. He handed five hundred dollars to me and walked away without saying a word.

A week later we played for the championship against the team sponsored by the Terrace Café. We won easily. Following our victory, we celebrated by having drinks and dinner right at the Terrace Café. The patrons and wait staff were good sports and gave us a standing ovation. One of the managers told me that his establishment was often frequented by Jack Cunningham. Jack wasn't there that night, but the manager assured me that the news of our celebration would definitely get back to him.

The bad blood between us continued into some business dealings

Cunningham operated a meat company called Fancy Foods that distributed poultry and a line of other products to Waldbaum's and some of the same supermarket chains where I sold my hamburgers. The Castellano family was heavily involved in this operation and had a strong connection to Jack Cunningham, to whom they provided the money to launch Fancy Foods. (4) A few of these other supermarkets asked me to sell my hamburgers directly to Fancy Foods and then let them handle the distribution to their stores. In this way the supermarkets would have to deal with only one vendor rather than two and still get the same products.

Because of the convenience and lower delivery costs to Topps, I reluctantly agreed to this plan, but I was leery about the arrangement from the beginning. First of all, I knew that Jack was involved with Big Pauley Castellano and payoffs to the supermarket chains. I had also heard about an incident involving one of Jack Cunningham's main competitors, a man named Arthur Salin, who was the owner of H & H Poultry, another main supplier of poultry to Waldbaum's. In May 1985 Salin was found murdered in the Bronx, New York, after having been shot in the head. The murder remains unsolved to this day. (3)

I never discussed this incident with Jack Cunningham or for that matter with any of my other connected friends. But I took note of the fact—perhaps coincidence—that in the aftermath of Salin's murder, Fancy Foods had become the principal distributor of poultry to Waldbaum's.

Early on in our business affiliation, Jack and I had many

disagreements. Our main dispute centered on the fact that his refrigerated trucks were not cold enough for my frozen hamburgers. He was also slow at paying his invoices and soon ran up a pretty big bill to Topps. I cut him off until I received a check.

Our relationship quickly disintegrated. I was convinced that we could not do business together; however, I received a call from Brooklyn asking me to go a little softer on Jack, to give him another chance. As usual the call came from an underling, but I knew it was a message from the top. The heads of the families never took a chance that their orders could be heard on a wiretapped call.

I tried to patch things up with Jack and move ahead under the terms of our original deal, but he refused to adhere to regular payment of my invoices. As a result, my relationship with him continued to deteriorate and became increasingly contentious.

Although I knew he was connected to some of the biggest Mob figures in Brooklyn, I didn't back off. I made it clear that there would be no further deliveries until he paid me in full.

Weeks went by, and the ill will continued. Frustrated by his arrogance and refusal to cooperate, I discontinued all business dealings with Jack Cunningham.

Finally things came to a head when our local meat association had a golf outing and dinner for its members. When the evening was over, many of us stood outside waiting for the valet to bring up our vehicles. The valet brought up my station wagon—a somewhat beat-up vehicle that I used for my business. As I was about to get behind the wheel, Jack's Corvette convertible arrived in the next lane.

In front of a large group of members, he yelled over to me. "Hey, Sachs, when you have my kind of money, you'll burn yours. Or maybe you'll get rid of that shit box and buy a decent car." Typical Jack Cunningham obnoxious comment.

Everyone laughed.

I just drove away.

Over the next few weeks, I heard rumors that Jack had become involved in the new and rapidly growing business of video cassette rentals. These same rumors indicated that he had switched his allegiance from his previous Mob connections in Brooklyn to a different Mob group in the Bronx. Jack was always lured by the chance to make a big score. However, I knew almost immediately that such changes in allegiance were often done at one's own peril.

The Mob did not just expect loyalty; it demanded it.

Several weeks later the story leaked out: Jack Cunningham was found dead in his Queens apartment. No details were provided, but rumors circulated, none of which were ever substantiated. Although I have no direct knowledge about Cunningham's death, people claimed there was a single bullet in his head and his body was tied with rope to a kitchen chair in a sitting position. Tape was said to be wrapped tightly around his face so that his nose was pressed flat and upwards, resembling that of a pig. Apparently the Mob had grown tired of Jack Cunningham's antics and disloyalty, and Jack Cunningham had not paid attention to the methods used by the Mob to teach someone a lesson.

One might think that such a sensational murder would be excellent fodder for the New York media or an investigative reporter, but his death was never reported in the newspapers. Nor did any details about his grizzly demise appear on television. The police investigation was kept under wraps and went nowhere. No one was questioned; no one was ever arrested. Just another unsolved homicide.

The Mob made sure the entire episode was kept out of the public eye. It had its way of guaranteeing that certain matters remained private, but the word spread quickly throughout the underworld. It passed from one connected guy to another, sometimes in a whisper or a private conversation.

The Mob had sent a clear message: greedy pigs get slaughtered.

CHAPTER 13

My Topps Meat Business

BY THE TIME I reached my thirties, I had placed most of my early experiences aside and was determined to be successful in business. After all, there comes a point when reality kicks in and you realize that you have to figure out a way to support yourself and make a decent living. After a back-and-forth history of working with my father in his meat business, I was finally entrenched at Topps and making every effort to maintain a good relationship with him.

It was not easy.

My father was a complicated person, at times capable of showing love and affection for the well-being of his children and at other times totally self-absorbed and with a nasty mean streak. Our relationship was best described as love-hate. I never ceased to be amazed at how quickly he could put his own needs ahead of all others, including his family. A great example of his self-absorption occurred when I was sixteen years old and had just earned my junior driver's license. I was riding in my father's step-van on our way to pick up a meat order—legs of beef, chucks, and flanks—at Queens Zeger Meats.

Although I knew my father's driver's license had been temporarily suspended, he was firmly ensconced behind the wheel in his typical manner of flaunting the law. As we cruised down Metropolitan Avenue, he drove right through a red light. Within seconds blue lights began flashing several cars behind us. My father panicked and immediately turned the van onto a side street. While the van was still moving, he yelled over to me, "Quick! Switch seats and get behind the wheel."

"What? While the van is moving?"

"Now!" he yelled.

I crawled over to the driver's seat as he slid underneath me into the passenger seat.

Within seconds, the NYPD cruiser—siren blaring and lights flashing—pulled up behind us.

The police officer got out of his car, approached the driver's side of the van, and motioned to me to open the door of the van. He gave me an incredulous look. "Were you driving this van all along, son?"

"Yes, sir," I said.

"You old enough to drive this van?"

I handed my license to him.

He studied it for a few seconds. "Son, this is a junior license. You're not allowed to drive a commercial vehicle until you are at least eighteen." He glared over to my father. "Are you his father?"

"Yes," my father said with a shrug of his shoulders. "He's just trying to help me out a little with my meat pickups at Flushing Zeger's."

"You should know better," the cop barked. "The kid's underage, goes through a red light, could have had an accident. Could have hurt someone. Who knows? And you just sit there? What kind of father are you?"

My father turned away and looked out the window. He said nothing.

I ended up with a citation, the loss of my junior license for three months, and a mark on my driving record.

My father never apologized or discussed the incident again.

My mother was very different. She was attractive; a wonderful cook; and a loving, caring person who always placed the best interests of her children as her number-one priority. Although she was subjected to physical abuse by my father, she never tried to turn her children against him. When she finally divorced him, we completely understood and were happy for her newfound freedom to move on in her life without fear.

The divorce settlement was a matter strictly between my parents, and they tried to keep the kids out of it, but I got wind of the terms and knew right away that my father was taking advantage of my mother. The initial offer to my mother was $5,000 cash and $75.00 a week—a ridiculous lowball offer.

I went to see my mother's lawyer. "The offer has to be higher," I said.

"What makes you say so? Do you have experience in divorce settlements?" he asked. The sarcastic look on his face was annoying.

I resisted the urge to reach across the desk and slug him. "No," I said, "but I know she's entitled to a larger settlement."

"How much larger?"

"Twenty-five thousand dollars cash and a hundred twenty-five dollars a week."

The lawyer looked stunned and sat back in his seat. He stared at me for a few seconds as he sized me up for making such an outlandish request. "You've got some balls to ask for that much," he said.

"Yes, I've got balls, but I've also got knowledge ... knowledge about how my father's been hiding money from the government all these years. So get on the phone with my father's lawyer and tell him what we know and what we want."

Within one week the terms were agreed upon and the divorce papers were filed. My mother received exactly what I asked for—$25,000 cash and $125.00 a week.

Despite my intervention in their divorce, my father never discussed it with me. I continued to work with him every day at Topps and made every effort to maintain a somewhat civil relationship; however, I kept a close eye on the checkbook to make sure that he made regular payments to my mother as stipulated in the divorce settlement. My mother always looked out for me; it was my small way of returning the favor.

My father had a myopic view of his business—Topps Meat. He was content with small local stores and restaurants that paid cash for their orders. Unfortunately these orders were never cash on delivery. They paid at the end of the week or, in some cases, at the end of the month. Since it was my job to collect the payments, I often got involved in having to chase down the owner to settle the bill. This task became tiresome, a real drag, and I hated having to spend Saturday nights showing up at a restaurant to corner the owner and inform him that next week's order of hamburger was not going to be delivered until he paid his overdue bill.

My father rationalized the inconvenience because he loved the cash. Furthermore, it was a business model that allowed him to hide some income, but this mindset kept him wallowed in mediocrity, trapped as a small-time operator.

I wanted to go big. I kept thinking about my conversation with Frank DeAngelis several years earlier. I wanted that big loaf of bread more than ever, but I didn't want to share it, and for sure, I didn't want to share it with the Mob.

My eyes were set on expanded manufacturing—selling to supermarkets, restaurant chains, wholesale stores, and institutions. As a result, my father and I were never on the same wavelength about the future of Topps. He wanted the comfortable status quo. I wanted to buy him out.

I approached him about a buyout, but he wanted $35,000 cash for a one-third share of the partnership. I had saved up about ten thousand dollars, but there was no way I could come up with the rest of the money, so I went back to working hard and tried to expand the business within the strict confines of my father's wishes. I hustled and picked up some pretty good accounts and began to think that my days of consorting with the Mob and its associates were over.

After high school I didn't have direct contact with most of my friends from my early days in Brooklyn. They had gone their way and I had gone my way. I heard more rumors and stories about some of their criminal activities—that they had joined with their fathers in illegal crimes, such as loan sharking, control of unions, and racketeering. I had decided to keep my distance and avoid initiating any contact that might complicate my business future, but every corner I turned seemed to lead me back to the Mob.

One of the new accounts happened to be Western Beef, and that company just happened to be owned by the Castellano family.

Yes, THE Castellano family.

Peter Castellano ("Petey"), who ran the business, was Paul ("Big Pauley") Castellano's cousin. Big Pauley was also involved in other meat companies and sold to retail and wholesale stores in and around Brooklyn. I eventually sold to all of these outlets, including many in Brooklyn, the Bronx, and Queens. As my business relationships with the Castellano family grew, my personal relationships with the Mob in Brooklyn grew as well. I was around Mob members often.

Frank DeAngelis invited me to a get-together. Frank and I had developed a very good relationship, and I always felt like he was looking out for my best interests. Along the way Frank helped me make some very important contacts and introduced me to many influential people in the Mob.

"Hey, Stevie," Frank said with his usual flamboyant flair. "Come over here! I want you to meet Charlie Anselmo."

Charlie Anselmo was a member of the Bonanno family and the leader of his own crew in the Bronx. He was about six feet tall, a burly, tough-looking, but handsome man. He had a great personality and the ability to take over a room when he just walked in. He loved to wear black and often reminded me of a movie actor in a Mafia-themed movie. Almost no one ever referred to him by his full name. He was simply Charlie A.

Charlie A had his hands in everything. He was a broker in the meat business and notorious for being an enforcer for the Mob at the 14th Street meat market. If you crossed the Mob in any way, you had to deal with Charlie A, and the penalty could be severe. At the end of one of these confrontations you might end up with smashed knuckles or broken legs but come away from it feeling thankful that you were still alive.

Charlie A was also a loan shark. If you needed money, he gladly loaned it to you, but the interest rate could be as high as five to ten percent *per week.* For these loans, the word on the street was very clear: don't even think of stalling Charlie A on repayment of your loan.

Charlie A looked at me with a big smile. "Nice to meet you, Steve. We know of you, mostly from Frank. But it's all good. I hear you're working your way up in the business. That's terrific." His outgoing, friendly manner was disarming.

I shook his hand and blurted out a one-word reply: "Thanks."

"Come around with Sonny P or Freddie Ruffino anytime

you're in the area," he said.

"I will."

"And of course that includes your friend, Johnny Lanoue."

I knew Freddie Ruffino from trade shows, and, through Freddie, I had gotten to know Sonny P. We got together socially on many occasions and had become good friends, but it was a bit disconcerting to know that Charlie A knew that I hung out with these guys, despite having been introduced to me only a few minutes earlier.

Johnny Lanoue? Haven't seen him in years. How does Charlie A know I know him?

Over time I learned that this was not unusual. Mob members made it their business to know who knew who. In this way they understood how people were connected, either by family, business, or otherwise. By knowing the connections, they were able to put pressure in the right places to get what they wanted. This knowledge base was an essential part of the formula for their success, a formula that no one understood better than Charlie A.

Many rumors and stories circulated about Charlie A. In some ways his escapades and criminal activities—many of which were chronicled in Jonathan Kwitny's 1979 best-selling documentary book, *Vicious Circles*—are the stuff of legends. In one year alone Charlie A was reported to have sold two million pounds of meat on the East Coast, a staggering amount by any measure. (4) Sales of that volume made him a true kingpin in the meat industry on a national scale.

But he was also accused of transporting and selling tainted meat—some of which was horsemeat and mink meat—as well as bribing meat inspectors to approve the shipments. (5) He was eventually indicted and sent to a minimum-security prison for a short four-and-a-half-month sentence. The word on the street was that Charlie A—a master of his craft—had worked out a deal with the judge that sentenced him, yet another example of the far-reaching, insidious impact of the Mob on everyday life in America.

Despite his sordid reputation, Charlie A and I eventually forged a very friendly and mutually respectful relationship. He was all personality—boisterous, gregarious, yet warmly engaging to those he liked. Soon after that first introduction, he knew even more details about my life and my dreams of buying out my father and expanding Topps into a major player in the meat industry. We became such good friends that he invited my family and me to his home for Christmas dinners. He also introduced me to executives at Waldbaum's, a major supermarket chain in New York, which became the first big supermarket account for Topps. Even though it wasn't another cash client, my father had to agree, because it was such a big deal.

During my early days in school, I had developed some artistic talent, so in 1976 I designed a red, white, and blue-striped box for packaging hamburgers in commemoration of the 200th anniversary of the Declaration of Independence. Charlie A loved the design and brought it to Victory Markets. Next thing I knew, we had another big contract.

With all of these new deals, I insisted that the brokerage pay by check after an invoice. In one of our many discussions, I made my feelings clear. "My business has to be on the up and up—totally legit," I said. "No under-the-table cash payments. I respect that you have a different take on these matters, but I have to run Topps in a straightforward business manner that will never come under scrutiny from the IRS."

Charlie smiled. "No problem, Stevie. I'll help you in any way I can, and you run your business any way you want." Charlie A never revisited this subject again.

Charlie A was high up in the Bonanno Family and introduced me to some of his friends in the Bronx and Westchester. Some of these guys were "made men"—fully initiated members of the Mob who had to prove their loyalty by carrying out a contract killing—the Mob's way of verifying that the inductee was not an undercover policeman. Despite their reputation and status within the Mob, I never had a problem with any of them. On Saturdays they often drove down to the Topps plant to pick up an order of shell steaks, chops, racks of lamb, and veal cutlets. Unlike most other encounters with their business associates who, out of fear, gave them free meat products, they never expected free meat from me. Instead I gave them a fair price and they paid for their orders. This relationship existed because I had gained the friendship and respect of Charlie A.

Charlie A and I had many lunches together. Usually we ate at Manganero's Restaurant on 9th Avenue and 38th Street, a place famous for being the home of the six-foot hero. He always wanted to eat at that Italian restaurant because it served tripe. I never let him know that I hated tripe. Not only did I hate the flavor, but at times even the odor got to me. However, on those occasions when tripe was on the menu, I put my personal tastes aside and ate tripe with Charlie A. It was my way of paying respect to him.

One day he called to say he wanted to meet for lunch at a different place, Giordano's Restaurant on 9th Avenue and 40th Street, a place famous for a flower garden right in the middle of the restaurant. Giordano's was also a favorite hangout for the Lucchese and Genovese Mob that together were major players in the garment and trucking industries.

As we sat in the restaurant, Charlie A looked over at me with a twinkle in his eye. "Stevie," he said, "are you still interested in buying out your old man?'

"Of course. But I don't have all the money I need. I've got two kids. Money is tight, and I'm thinking of buying a house. To buy out one-third of my father, I still have to come up with $25,000."

Gradually he used his leg to push something on the floor toward me. "Pick up this bag, but don't be too conspicuous about it," he said.

I waited a minute, looked around to make sure no one was paying attention, and then reached down and picked up the bag.

Charlie A. had a sheepish grin on his face. "Take a look in there, and don't say too much about the contents," he said.

I slowly opened the bag and glanced inside. I looked away for a few seconds and then peered into the bag again. I counted to myself. The bag contained twenty-five packs of one hundred-dollar bills, ten to a pack. A total of $25,000 in cash.

I shook my head and looked over at Charlie A. "Charlie," I said, "I appreciate the offer, but I can't afford the vig on this loan."

"There's no vig," he said.

I stared at him in disbelief.

"In fact," he said, "there's no interest, no points, and no re-payment schedule. The guys got together and threw some money into a pot for you. You deserve it, kid. Pay the money back someday when you have it. Not a penny more than the twenty-five K."

To this day I still get tears in my eyes thinking back to that moment.

Within a year, however, through hard work—literally hustling and busting my ass every day—I was able to pay that money back completely.

This was just another way in which I was able to gain the

trust and respect of members of the Mob.

Years later, while attending a wedding with his wife, Charlie Anselmo had a massive heart attack and fell dead on the dance floor. The headlines read: Ruthless, Notorious Mob Figure Dies Suddenly.

Those headlines hardly described the Charlie Anselmo I knew and loved.

CHAPTER 14

The Monarch

IN 1975 I was living in The Whitehall in Riverdale, New York, with my wife, baby girl, and son. The Whitehall was and still is a premier apartment residence in New York located a short drive from Manhattan and offering picturesque views of the Manhattan skyline and the Hudson River.

At that time the building was occupied by quite a few celebrities and former athletes, including Hall of Famer Willie Mays, the actress Yvonne DiCarlo, and the Yankees' Bobby Murcer, among many others.

The building also had its share of infamous people, including Leroy (Nicky) Barnes, the corrupt drug kingpin of Harlem. Nicky had a long rap sheet that included drug convictions that resulted in a three-year stretch of imprisonment in The Tombs—yes, the same Tombs I described in previous chapters.

Along the way, while doing another prison sentence at Green Haven State Prison, he befriended Mafia crime boss "Crazy" Joey Gallo, a member of the Colombo family and Matthew Madonna, a member of the Lucchese crime family. According to later trial records, Gallo was interested in expanding his criminal empire into the Harlem heroin business. When Gallo was released from prison, he provided a high-priced lawyer for

Nicky Barnes, whose conviction was eventually overturned on a technicality.

Once Barnes was set free from prison in the early 1970s, he established an African-American drug-distribution enterprise based on the Mafia business model in which the leaders, known as The Council, controlled all decisions made by an intricate and expansive illegal operation. In a short span of several years, Nicky Barnes became fabulously rich and moved into The Whitehall. I saw him a few times. He was always dressed in a flamboyant style—fur coats, gold jewelry, and fancy Italian shoes. We exchanged cordial hellos, but the conversations never went further than that. I knew of his reputation and connections; I preferred to keep my distance, while at the same time keeping my connections to myself.

Nicky also drove expensive cars, of which he had three—a Bentley, a Maserati, and a Mercedes-Benz. Rumors swirled around him and he was estimated to be worth $50 million. He even appeared on the cover of *New York Magazine* under the caption, Mr. Untouchable, a nickname earned because it seemed that the Feds could never build a successful case against him.

The DEA, however, finally caught up to Leroy "Nicky" Barnes. One day FBI agents showed up at The Whitehall armed with automatic rifles and wearing bullet-proof vests.

I stood back and watched the scene unfold from a distance.

Nicky Barnes was taken away in handcuffs.

In 1977 he was convicted of racketeering and a slew of drug-related crimes and sentenced to life in prison without parole. Thus "Mr. Untouchable" moved from The Whitehall to the Big House.

I never saw him again.

In his later years Nicky turned state's evidence and

cooperated with then U.S. Attorney Rudi Giuliani to testify against his former associates, eleven of whom were convicted and sentenced to long prison terms. As a result of his cooperation, Nicky's sentence was reduced from life without parole to thirty-five years. He died of natural causes while living under the Witness Protection Program.

My favorite acquaintance at The Whitehall, however, was Richie Shariff, a guy who was also known as The Monarch. Richie had contracted polio at an early age and had been in a wheelchair since he was five years old. But his disability never hindered his inner drive for success. He inherited two newspaper routes from his father and hired a few young boys to handle the deliveries. The routes provided his basic income.

His most lucrative source of income, however, came from poker. Richie was an extraordinary poker player—so good that if he were alive today, he would easily be one of the top players in Las Vegas.

Richie not only played poker, but he also ran several big poker games, one of which took place right in a card room at The Whitehall. Richie provided a venue for the game as well as supplying the food and drinks for the participants who paid a small fee for the refreshments. The drinks were soda, iced tea, and water. No alcohol.

Richie ran the game, but unlike most poker organizers, he took no percentage of each pot for himself. He didn't have to; he simply relied on his poker skills to come out ahead. When Richie reeled in a large pot, the other players often said, "The Monarch strikes again," true testament to the respect he enjoyed from the other players.

I got to know Richie as one of the players, and we soon became friends. Before long he recruited me to be his assistant in running the poker games.

The players came from all walks of life—celebrities, actors, doctors, lawyers—but they were serious players who didn't shy away from a big money game. Every pot in these games was between $2,000 and $6,000—a substantial sum in 1975. A player could easily lose $25,000 in one night. The poker games in The Whitehall sometimes started on a Thursday night and ran through late Sunday afternoon. It was a marathon gambling experience.

The games had a steady group of players, but the length of the games occasionally caused someone to step out for a day. In those instances, we had no problem finding an alternate player to join the game. The word had gotten around that Richie's poker game was the place to be.

Sometimes we ran two games at the same time. The demand for this high- stakes action was really incredible.

There was a small kitchen next to the card room at The Whitehall. I used it to broil filet mignon, and at the usual 8:30 p.m. break, I made filet sandwiches for the players.

Despite the high stakes and the possibility of losing a lot of money, the players got along very well. Those poker nights were as much a social occasion as they were an opportunity to showcase your ability to call someone's bluff. The players were comprised of men and women, and all the women were respected. In Richie Shariff's poker group, no swearing or foul language was allowed if women were in the game. If a player violated this rule, Richie quickly called him out. If such behavior continued, the player would not be invited to play again.

The Monarch's game was honest—skill and knowledge of poker were the determining factors in who ended up in the win column and who lost a bundle of cash. All the regular players came to the game knowing it was possible to lose $100,000 or more in a year, but the players were all pretty well-heeled when it came to money.

One of the regular players was a woman named Janet who owned a string of motels in New Jersey. We are friends to this day.

Another woman was the daughter of a major bookie in London and also owned several brownstones on 8th Avenue in the city. She knew all about gambling and had the money to back her addiction to poker. When she came to New York at the end of the month to collect her rents, she always showed up at our poker game.

We also had a few guys who were heavy hitters in the financial world. They knew how to take calculated risks, and poker was a logical outlet for their daring tendencies, for which they often reaped handsome rewards. But the thrill of making a big score also led them to dabble in cocaine, a risk they never should have taken. Week after week I studied their behavior and noticed a significant change in their betting patterns after the 8:30 break. They tended to make poor decisions, and at times seemed to be unaware of which cards had been played. I knew their problems weren't related to my steak sandwiches; rather it was the blow of cocaine they were sniffing in the men's room.

If Janet was losing money early in the game, I always advised her to be patient, because those guys would give back all their winnings and then some within an hour or so of resuming play after the break.

I was right.

Janet and I often winked at each other after she called one of their bluffs and raked in a large pile of chips.

One day Richie came to me with an idea to run a Casino Night for charities. "Steve," he said, "my father had a friend who's a local councilman. I'm gonna contact him about getting a permit to run this thing. You wanna help?"

"Sure, Richie. Anything I can do."

Within two weeks we had a permit and were up and running. I assumed Richie had to grease a palm or two to get such a fast approval, but I never asked.

We brought in tables for roulette, blackjack, craps, and poker. The entire venture was wildly successful, and we expanded it to twice a month. The charities that benefitted included the Fire and Police Department Pension Funds, the Police Athletic League, the YMCA, and the Heart Foundation, all charities that the local politicians favored for their own selfish reasons. These political hacks had the audacity to brag and take credit for helping the charities gain more funding. And, of course, Richie had to pay off some of these same politicians to keep our permitting license renewed every month.

Richie worked hard and deserved to be compensated for his time and efforts to keep his venture going. He considered his fee to be part of the overhead expenses to run the events. Through these Casino Nights, during which he did not play poker, he helped the charities, did well for himself, and even threw a few hundred a month to me for my assistance. Within a year, however, the local politicians smelled the money and became too greedy. They wanted a bigger piece of the net. Paying them more graft meant paying much less to the charities. We tried to reason with these crooked officials, but got nowhere. They were as bad as the Mob when it came to making demands for brokerage fees. Maybe worse.

Frustrated with these negotiations, Richie and I decided to shut down Casino Night.

In the end, between the money I won playing poker at The Whitehall and the pay I received for helping Richie, I was able to put together enough cash for a deposit on a house in Rivervale, New Jersey.

Through all of this, my most important takeaway was that Richie Shariff, The Monarch—a title well deserved—was my poker mentor.

We spent hours talking about poker strategy and discussing various poker hands that could have been handled differently—a check, a call, or a raise that would have changed the outcome. He taught me everything I know about the game and made me a winner.

Richie Shariff was indeed a special guy. I miss him. He passed away too young—in his forties—from pulmonary complications arising from his disability.

I think of him often when I reach across a poker table and haul in a large pot.

CHAPTER 15

Rivervale, New Jersey

IN 1979 I moved my family from The Whitehall apartment residence in Riverdale, New York to our first home in the small town of Rivervale, New Jersey. The move was much more than simply changing one letter in the town's name. Unlike the traffic and congestion we faced in New York, Rivervale was quiet and serene.

We found a new community that was being developed just a few streets away from Rivervale Road. Eighty percent of this community—of which only three streets were developed at that time—was composed of young Jewish families. We felt comfortable in our new neighborhood, signed the kids up for school, and settled in.

For the first three months everything was perfect, but the peace and tranquility were short-lived. One night at 9:30 the doorbell rang. The sound woke up the kids. I went to the door and looked out.

Nobody was there.

The next morning I looked out and saw swastikas marked in white chalk in the street and on the front of some of the driveways. Some of the neighbors had already congregated on the street, so I walked out to join them. Only the homes of families with Jewish names were affected.

This area of New Jersey was known to have members of the German American Bund, an organization of Nazi sympathizers in the late 1930s. Although the organization itself fell apart during World War II and its leaders were imprisoned and later deported, remnants of anti-Semitism persisted.

We all agreed that the incident was more than just a few pranksters enjoying a bit of vandalism.

It was a definite message.

However, the group chose to consider it an isolated incident—perhaps high schoolers with nothing better to do. They decided to avoid giving it more attention by filing a police report, so they did nothing.

I disagreed and warned that action was required to prevent further incidents from occurring. In an informal show of hands, my suggestion was overruled.

Two nights later the same pattern occurred—doorbells rung late at night; chalk-marked swastikas found on driveways and the street in the morning.

This second act prompted a neighborhood meeting at the home of one of the neighbors the next evening. The general feeling of the homeowners was that a police report should be filed, but publicity of the events should be avoided out of fear that it might affect the property values of the homes and discourage new buyers from moving into our development.

I knew this approach would never work.

For a few nights a police cruiser made some slow passes on our streets.

Nothing happened. No perpetrators were apprehended.

Four nights later, the police details stopped.

Two nights after that, the anti-Semitic vandalism resumed. Doorbells were rung even later at night. All the kids were awakened. Swastikas were once again painted on the streets and driveways.

A second meeting was called. I stood up and voiced my opinion. "We need a night patrol to catch these people and show them that this type of behavior will not be tolerated," I said.

A woman got up from her chair. "And who will make up this night patrol?"

"Us," I said, "the people who are the victims of these anti-Semitic attacks."

A lot of mumbling could be heard in the room. No one stood up to support my proposal. Finally a few people—the educated elite, I assumed—voiced their opinions: Night patrols would only antagonize the perpetrators and create more problems. Better to stay out of it and let the police take care of this issue.

I knew what would come by sitting back and ignoring anti-Semitism. I decided to handle this problem myself. Two nights later, my wife was upstairs getting our kids ready for sleep. I dressed all in black—shirt, pants, and a longshoreman's hat. I also painted my face with black boot polish. I sneaked out the back door of our house and walked into a small wooded area that separated the streets. I hid in the bushes and waited.

Within minutes I realized that my hiding place was also a location that dogs and cats used to relieve themselves. Many bugs had found this spot as well. My mind flashed back to the days when, as an eight-year-old kid, I used to hide in garbage cans. I almost broke out laughing at myself.

But I was determined.

I waited.

Sure enough, about 9:30, two large teenagers—muscular, athletic-looking guys who appeared to be seventeen or older—walked down our street and kneeled down in front of one of the driveways. They took white chalk out of their jackets and began drawing swastikas on the asphalt.

I stormed out of the woods and startled both of them. Before the bigger of the two could stand up, I hit him with a forearm to the side of his neck. He went down on the street coughing and gasping for breath. When he turned to look up at me, blood streamed down his face from the cut he sustained when his head hit the pavement. He was dazed.

The other kid got scared, and in his haste to make a fast get-away, tripped over his feet and fell on the curb. I grabbed him by his hair to pull him up. As he fought to resist, he scraped his lips and chin on the curb.

I let go of the guy, and they both ran off like scared rabbits.

I knew their injuries were superficial but enough to require an explanation when they got home or got on the school bus the next morning.

The next day the police went door to door asking questions. There were no witnesses. No one could provide an account of what happened.

When my son got home from school that day, he told me he had seen two of the older kids on the school bus with scrapes on their faces.

I just winked at him and said nothing.

He laughed.

Our neighborhood never had another incident with anti-Semitic graffiti painted on the streets. No more doorbells were rung late at night.

Our street was quiet and serene once again.

CHAPTER 16

38th Street

DURING MY LIFE I had several nicknames. One of them was Batman, not because I wore a mask and a cape and drove a Batmobile, but because my baseball bat bore the DNA of eight guys who committed crimes on 38th Street and 9th Avenue in New York City in the mid-1970s. It was "my" street, and I was determined to protect it.

At that time, 38th Street between 8th and 9th avenues belonged to the Midtown South Police Precinct. If you headed west and crossed over 9th Avenue toward Tenth Avenue, you entered the Tenth Police Precinct, commonly referred to as the Crooked Precinct. That's where my lockups began. But I'll get to that later.

One day I received a phone call at my meat plant. It was from the priest of the church on 40th Street. "Steve, this is Monsignor Walsh from St. Anthony's," he said.

"Yes, Father, what can I do for you?"

"I've called a lunchtime meeting at Giordano's restaurant, and I'd like you to attend."

"A meeting? Who's coming to this meeting?"

"I've invited Sal and Joe Manganero; Jimmy, the Nursery Guy; and the brothers from Vinny's Fruit Market. They're members of our parish here at St. Anthony's."

I recognized every name. Not only were they my friends and highly respected fellow businessmen in my area, but like me, they were tough guys with "connections." But I was still puzzled by the Monsignor's call. "Father, with all due respect, I'm Jewish. Why are you calling me?"

He laughed. "I know your reputation as a pretty tough guy, Steve. I need some tough guys to take care of a problem we have."

"What kind of a problem?"

"I've had enough of the crime and drugs that have infiltrated our neighborhood. The pushers, runners, and dealers are corrupting the lives of our young children who cross 38th and 9th on their way to parochial school."

"Have you talked to the police?"

"Yes, but I got nowhere. They're ignoring the situation. I think they've all been paid off."

I agreed to attend.

A few days later we sat at a large table in the rear of Giordano's restaurant and listened, Jimmy, the Nursery Guy; brothers Sal and Joe Manganero; and me, the only Jewish guy in the group.

Monsignor Walsh was a distinguished-looking man about fifty years old. He wore rimless glasses and sported thick, white hair perfectly coiffed. "Today I'm asking all of you for a favor," Monsignor Walsh started. "I need you guys to protect our children from this scourge of drugs. The children are suffering. Their mothers are crying. The police are doing nothing. Something needs to be done."

We sat silently, almost transfixed by his appeal.

"You've got to get these drug dealers out of our neighborhood. I don't care how you do it," he continued, his voice cracking with emotion. "When you're finished, I don't need the details." He looked away for a few seconds as he tried to compose himself. Coming from a man of the cloth, his unabashed candor on such a serious matter was stunning, but he had made a powerful, compelling case. The cops were doing nothing; it was our duty to take action ourselves.

The outcome of the meeting was no surprise. We looked at each other, nodded, and then told Monsignor Walsh that we would rid the area of these "animals" no matter what measures it took.

A period began that can be described as either controlled violence or complete chaos, whatever terms fit.

Jimmy owned the nursery off the corner of 38th and 9th only about one hundred feet from my meat plant. He was big, muscular, and fearless, the kind of guy you just didn't mess with. He became our eyes and ears on 9th Avenue from seven a.m. to six p.m.

I did the same, except I started at four a.m. and never stopped until I fell asleep at night. I hated those animals and was committed to driving them out of our area.

One morning at 7:15 Jimmy and I spotted a dark sedan with heavily tinted windows parked on 40th Street about a half block away from the church. The motor was running. A young boy no more than thirteen or fourteen approached the driver's side of the car. The window rolled down. The driver's arm reached out and handed a small package to the boy. The boy glanced around and then sprinted away.

Jimmy and I walked over to the car and tapped on the driver's side window. No response.

I tapped harder.

Still no response.

Finally I lifted my bat and smashed the barrel of the bat

through the window.

The driver, the sole occupant, recoiled in his seat and ducked his head as shards of glass showered toward his face and over his clothes. "What the fuck, man! Whaddya doin' here?"

"I'm sending you a message," I yelled.

The man had a wild-eyed look and leaned away toward the passenger seat, trying to distance himself from another attack with the bat. Ripples of blood trickled down on his face from several cuts. "Who the fuck are you? Why are you hasslin' me?"

I swung the bat again, this time smashing the rear passenger window. "Get out of this neighborhood and don't ever come back. If you do, I'll be breaking your legs instead of your windows," I said.

Jimmy leaned in with a sarcastic smile and issued a final warning. "And I'll make sure you lose a few teeth."

The man straightened up in his seat, shifted the car into drive, and peeled out of his parking space in a flash.

In a matter of months, using similar techniques, my crew and I had eliminated those scumbags from four city blocks that abutted 9th Avenue. Not only were our measures extremely effective, but they also had the full blessings of Monsignor Walsh, who applauded the results. As promised, he never asked how we achieved them.

We even took it upon ourselves to "dismiss" other undesirables whose behavior was not acceptable. Some of the drug addicts took part-time jobs pushing clothing racks to a warehouse after the clothes were unloaded from delivery trucks owned by Consolidated Carriers, Cord Trucking, or Art-Ed Trucking. All these trucking firms were either owned or controlled by the Mob. Many times these addicts stopped and urinated on the street or against a steel roll-up door at the entry of Bor-Air Freight's clothing warehouse. No matter how often I yelled and tried to chase them away, they ignored me and continued their obnoxious behavior.

I decided to take matters into my own hands. One day I heard the loud clatter of the clothing rack wheels as they were being pushed down the street. Immediately I knew a delivery truck had arrived and was being unloaded. I watched as two lowlifes pushed their clothing racks containing expensive furs from a red delivery truck toward the warehouse. I knew that all the trucks from Consolidated Carriers were red and that the company was owned by Joseph and Thomas Gambino, sons of Carlo Gambino.

Suddenly the two men paused and looked at each other. Then, in an apparent act of defiance, they unzipped their pants and began urinating on the steel door. They stood with their backs toward me, laughing the entire time, obviously enjoying their own form of bold resistance to authority.

I reached into one of the 250-pound steel drums that contained remnants of shin bones from cattle carcasses in my meat plant. Each shin bone weighed approximately eight pounds. I lifted two shin bones out of the drum, quietly walked across the street, and stood behind the two men. Without making a sound I threw the two shin bones against the top portion of the steel door, one after the other in rapid succession. Two loud, booming noises reverberated onto the street like an explosion of gunfire. Jolted by the sudden noise, the two men recoiled from the door and ducked their heads in fear.

"Holy shit!" one of them yelled.

"Let's get outta here," the other cried.

Without zipping up their pants, they ran down the street like scared rabbits, their private parts dangling in open air as they turned up 38th Street.

I paused for a few seconds to enjoy the comic scene that

had just unfolded before me. I then pushed the two clothing racks into my meat storage coolers and covered them with plastic to keep stray fibers from contaminating my hanging beef.

Fortunately when the meat inspectors came to my plant, they just rolled their eyes and never asked for an explanation. No fines were levied, and I never received a citation. But they suggested—with a smile—that I move the garments off the premises.

Eventually I received a call from one of the bosses at Consolidated Carriers looking for his merchandise. My conversation in these calls was always pretty straightforward: "You can pick up your garments provided that the guys who urinated on our street are banned from returning here for six months. And don't send them to do the pickup. Send two other guys."

The ground rules had been clearly established; there was no argument, no repercussions. Over a period of time, I began to understand that the Gambino brothers respected my position and shared my intolerance for such lascivious public behavior. In fact, after one such exchange, the trucking boss invited me to join him for lunch at Giordano's Restaurant.

In another incident, to beat the backed-up traffic a Hell's Angel drove his motorcycle on the sidewalk on his way to his job at a corrugated box company on my block. I stopped him several times and warned him that he was creating a danger to the children who were on their way to school, but he ignored my warnings and continued to drive his motorcycle on the sidewalk.

One morning when I heard his motorcycle, I grabbed my bat, stepped out of my doorway, and shoved the bat into the spokes of his front wheel. The startled guy flew off over the handlebars and landed in the street. He sprawled awkwardly on the pavement and then rolled over on his back. He glanced down at the sleeves of his black leather jacket that were torn near the elbows. "What the fuck?" he shouted. He looked up at me with an angry glare.

I stepped closer and issued a final warning. "Don't get up too fast, or I'll use this bat to beat the shit out of you."

He struggled to get to his feet, eyeing me warily the entire time. He mounted his motorcycle and began to drive away. When he was far enough away that I couldn't reach him with my bat, he paused and shouted, "I'll be back with my friends. We're gonna burn down your fuckin' building."

I lifted my bat and pointed it at him. "I'll be waiting for you," I said.

I took his threat seriously, though, and decided to take preemptive action. I made some inquiries and found out that Hell's Angels had its headquarters between 2nd Avenue and East 3rd Street. I also learned that its leader was a guy named Big Mike.

I drove down to the area, parked my truck, and walked up to a brownstone building that had bikers everywhere—on the street, on the steps, and on the sidewalks.

"Where's your leader?" I asked a young guy who sat on the steps.

He looked up with a quizzical expression. "Who are you?"

"That doesn't matter. Just take me to Big Mike."

Another young guy immediately joined him. They escorted me inside and frisked me. Since I never "carried" outside my office, there was no weapon to be found.

Suddenly the room was filled with a dozen other bikers, including the guy I had tripped off his cycle. Reinforcements for sure. They gathered around me in an intimidating manner, blocking my exit to the door. I had doubts that I would leave the room unscathed.

The first young guy that I had encountered outside looked

over to a grossly overweight man sitting in a large, soft arm-chair. "He's clean, Mike," he said.

Big Mike looked at me and smiled. "You've got big balls coming in here. But I like that," he said.

I stared him down for a few seconds and then nodded in agreement. "One of your stupid bikers kept riding on the side-walk, even when women and children were walking to school. I told him to stop, but he wouldn't listen. I had to teach him a lesson."

Big Mike looked around at the assembled group of men who stood rigidly, obviously waiting for his command to take action against me. He seemed to be sizing up his own crew, measuring their reaction to my bold statement. He looked back at me and issued his own warning. "Bikes are for the streets and highways. I agree with you; he was out of line," he said.

I glanced over to the assembled onlookers, taking a mea-sured look at the biker I had tripped. I turned back to Big Mike. "Before I leave, I need to know if we have a further problem."

Big Mike looked puzzled. "What further problem?"

"You gonna burn down my building?" I asked.

He stared at the group of bikers for a few seconds and then turned back to me. He smiled. "No, man. We're good."

I turned around.

The group of bikers cleared a path as I walked out the door.

CHAPTER 17

38ᵗʰ Street Part Two

MY EARLY DAYS as a protector of 38ᵗʰ Street from the influence of drugs and crime had a lasting effect on me. I hated those drug pushers for the negative impact they had on our neighborhood and especially for the way they ruined the lives of young people in the community.

I always kept my ear to the ground when it came to news about 38ᵗʰ Street. I talked to the regulars who frequented the area and found out that the drug pushers had developed a secret system for distribution of their drugs. As a result of this system, they never could get arrested for handing the drugs over to a buyer in exchange for money. Their system was ingenious in a way, but they never planned on my ability to destroy it.

The electric lampposts along 9ᵗʰ Avenue had a triangular flap at the base that was held to the post by several Phillips screws. The inside of the base was hollow. The drug pushers removed the two lower screws so the triangular flap could be simply swung upward to open. In the middle of the night, at two, three, or four o'clock in the morning, young children—preteens—placed colored bags—red, green, white, yellow, etc.—inside the bases of a number of lampposts. The bags were filled with varying amounts of drugs. The drug pushers used young children for this task because the kids could never be prosecuted if arrested. A little later, when the drug buyers showed up, the pushers collected their money and told the buyer which lamppost and which colored bag contained the drugs they purchased.

On a few early mornings I took it upon myself to watch these transactions taking place and noticed there was never a cop around to interfere. Of course, the police in question belonged to the Tenth Precinct, so I never expected anything less. The drug dealers owned them, and everybody knew it.

I decided to take action. I had a one-hundred-foot hose in my plant. One morning, just before five a.m., I hooked it up to the spigot inside and dragged it up 38th Street to the corner of 9th Avenue. I lifted the flaps on several lampposts. Three bags—red, green and white—were inside each base. I turned my hose nozzle to jet spray and flooded the bases with water. The force of the spray caused some of the bags to break open. Pills and capsules scattered all over the street and ran into the gutters. The stream of water carried many of the pills into the sewer drain, rendering the cache of illegal drugs totally useless.

I dragged the hose back to my store. I had a cup of coffee and stayed alert, watching for the outcome of my mischief. Sure enough, at six a.m., before daybreak, several guys showed up and seemed to be milling around the flooded lampposts. They bent down and looked all around and inside the bases of the lampposts. They had a look of confusion, and then they walked away.

Within minutes they returned and were accompanied by another car. The driver of the second car also inspected the area around the lampposts.

If I could have read his mind, he'd be wondering, *Who the fuck did this?*

After a heated discussion with the first few guys, I spotted him handing something back to each one of them; obviously a refund.

Early the next morning at five a.m., the area was calm. No pedestrian traffic or other visitors to the lampposts off 38th Street. I walked up to 9th Avenue and looked around. I saw two guys leaning over a lamppost a little farther down on 9th Avenue. They removed a small bag. It was clear to me that the drug pushers had simply relocated their operation to a few lampposts on the other side of 9th Avenue.

Later that morning I drove over to Sears and purchased two hundred more feet of hose and connected it to my existing hundred-foot hose.

At four a.m. the next morning, I crossed to the west side of 9th Avenue and flooded about a half dozen lamppost stashes of paper bags full of illegal drugs. However, I was then on the side of the street that was under the jurisdiction of the Tenth Police Precinct. Again, the street and gutters were awash with a stream of pills and capsules. I was having so much fun that I couldn't contain my laughter.

Suddenly the sound of sirens and the sight of flashing blue lights interrupted my fun. The Tenth Precinct cops, tipped off by the drug pushers, had arrived to arrest me. They cuffed me, rattled off a list of charges, and put me into the back of a cruiser.

"Will you guys roll up my hose and put it back in front of my plant? I think I'm going to be unavailable for a few hours," I said.

The sergeant gave me an annoyed sneer, shoved me by the shoulder, and slammed the door closed. The cops took me to the holding cell of the Tenth Precinct and booked me on several misdemeanor charges. I was told that I had to wait until later in the morning for an appearance before a judge. But long before my hearing, the captain of the Midtown South Precinct, Jack

Peace, called the captain of the Tenth Precinct and gave him a simple message: "Steve Sachs is one of our guys. Let him go."

And they did.

Altogether I was eventually arrested three times by the Tenth Precinct cops for attempting to destroy public property. What the citation should have stated is that I was interfering with the normal, everyday commerce of the 9th Avenue drug pushers who provided a major source of income for the Tenth Precinct police force.

The cops got rough with me. Punches were thrown; nightsticks were jabbed into my ribcage; and, yes, I responded by defending myself and punching out a few of the cops. Finally, to teach a lesson to me, I was thrown into The Tombs so I could stew for a while before presenting my case to a judge.

And maybe, while I was there, something unpleasant might happen to me?

But I had an ace in the hole named Rosie. She was the secretary for Jack Peace, the captain of Midtown South. Whenever I was in the middle of an issue with the drug pushers on 38th and 9th and the Tenth Precinct cops, I called Rosie and asked her to update her boss on my status.

Rosie always came through for me, and that's why Rosie received a dozen roses from me every two months.

Within a few hours Jack Peace made a call to the captain at the Tenth Precinct, and I was set free, but not before I had become the new friend of a huge guy named Tiny.

Now you know the rest of my story about The Tombs.

CHAPTER 18

Dracula Landlord

FOR ABOUT FOUR months it was peaceful on 9th Avenue. Apparently, our informal vigilante committee had done a good job in discouraging the drug pushers from continuing their business operation in our community.

One of my favorite eating places was Guido's on 9th Avenue. In the 1920s Guido's was a grocery store before it became known as the Supreme Macaroni Company.

But it was much more than a grocery store. It was a true Italian delicatessen. One of its distinguishing features was the full line of rabbits that hung from hooks in the front window. As customers walked in, they passed pullout bins full of imported pasta and a wide variety of imported cans of tomato paste and olive oil. The Supreme Macaroni Company prospered and became a landmark business in New York.

The store also became a hangout for the Lucchese and Genovese crime families. Between 1920 and 1940, Mama Guido cooked special meals for the members and associates in the back of the grocery store where they could enjoy her incredible pasta dishes out of view of other customers and, in particular, safely away from rival families and FBI agents that had them under constant surveillance.

In later years, as the older members of the Mob families either died or were sent to prison, Mama Guido decided to renovate the grocery store and convert it into an Italian restaurant.

Today it is operated by her grandchildren and is still known as one of New York City's most famous restaurants.

As I walked out of Guido's after a delicious lunch, I passed by a few of the brownstone apartment buildings on the Tenth Precinct side of 38th Street and 9th Avenue. Although I had heard that these buildings were recently purchased and scheduled for renovations, I had no other information. Several workmen were busy outside and taking orders from a man dressed completely in black clothing. I instantly recognized him from newspaper reports in *The New York Post* and the *Daily News*.

He was the Dracula Landlord.

His real name was Leonard Spodek, and he had an infamous reputation for owning large apartment buildings in Brooklyn and the Bronx and allowing them to fall into disrepair. As a result, older tenants whose apartment had been under rent control moved out, thus clearing the way for the Dracula Landlord to legally increase the rent. Rumors also circulated that some of the apartments were being rented to drug gangs that used the apartment as a headquarters for their illegal drug operations.

The presence of the drug gangs also served as encouragement for other tenants to vacate the building, opening up even more apartments for rent increases.

Just when we thought we had cleaned up the neighborhood, an entire new group of gang-related drug pushers had taken occupancy, posing another threat to the good families in the neighborhood.

I contacted my neighborhood vigilantes and set up a meeting to discuss a plan of action. We resumed our "watch" patrol, looking out early in the mornings for parked cars with occupants who were visited by people obviously making drug transactions. Some of the visitors were young people, teenagers who fit the profile of those who often got hooked and then became drug pushers themselves.

Our group worked in pairs, sometimes in threes, as we approached the parked cars as early as 4:30 in the morning. If the driver locked the doors and didn't get out of the car, we'd simply smash the window, unlock the car, and drag him out. From that point on it was a matter of how much of a beating the drug pusher was willing to accept before promising to leave and never return.

Once our message was firmly delivered and an agreement reached, I always finished the encounter by leaving him with a lasting economic consideration. I made sure that the drugs in his possession were rendered useless by unscrewing the gas cap and pouring them into the gasoline tank of his car.

We always left the scene before the Tenth Precinct cops could be notified and I could be arrested again.

The drug-pushing hierarchy didn't appreciate our attacks on its sales team. Our neighborhood patrol group became a target of revenge. Interestingly enough, it had a willing accomplice.

One morning I parked my car in a space I rented on 37th Street, a parking area inside the Tenth Precinct. As I got out of the car to begin the walk to my plant, I was jumped by three guys. A vicious fist fight ensued. I didn't recognize any of the men who were attacking me. No reason was given. No attempt was made to steal my wallet or grab the keys to my car.

I couldn't get to my bat. I had to rely on my fists to keep from being bludgeoned by the guys. I held my ground and fought them off, but I took a fair number of punches in the process.

Within minutes the Tenth Precinct cops appeared, cuffed

me, and told the guys who jumped me to stop making trouble and get on their way. The cops didn't even bother to take their names. I realized it was a setup and just another excuse to send me to The Tombs.

CHAPTER **19**

Pork Spleens

IN THE SPRING of 1980, I was in the midst of intense negotiations to buy my father's remaining interest in Topps Meat. He had been spending more time vacationing in Florida and had made it clear that he was interested in retiring. However, negotiating with my father was no easy task. Each of us had a team of lawyers to work out the details of the deal, the final cost of which was complicated by my father's shady attempts to jack up the price.

His efforts to increase monthly profits and thus raise the value of the buyout took on a new level of compulsive behavior that far exceeded his previous transgressions.

In short, he ventured into outright illegal measures to make money.

I returned to Topps after a two-week vacation of my own. As per my usual routine, I did a survey of our inventory in the four stories of meat freezers that were located in our warehouse on 38th Street. In the fourth-floor meat freezer, I found our usual large order of Australian boneless chuck, the main ingredient of our hamburger patties. However, something about the storage of the order caught my attention. The palettes holding the boxes were stacked in a somewhat unusual manner.

I climbed up on the palettes and stretched over the top layer to look behind the boxes. I shined my flashlight downward to get a better look at the inventory that was covered—*concealed* is a more appropriate word—by the Australian boneless chuck. I discovered a large supply of boxes that were totally unfamiliar.

I crawled over the top layer of boxes and stretched farther down to catch a glimpse of the packing label on one of the strange boxes, all of which were positioned so the label could not be easily read. The packing label read "Pork Spleens."

Why are these boxes in our warehouse?

I counted the boxes. All together there were eight hundred boxes, each containing thirty pounds of pork spleens.

Twelve tons of pork spleens!

I immediately grasped the gravity of this situation. My father planned to use the pork spleens as an unlisted ingredient, or "filler", in our hamburger-manufacturing process. The inexpensive product would reduce our overhead cost significantly and greatly improve the profit line of every pound of hamburger meat we sold.

There was just one problem: the practice was illegal.

I went back to the office. I rifled through all the current invoices, hoping that my father had not paid it while I was away. I found it. Luckily the invoice had not been paid.

I walked into the plant and confronted my father, almost shoving the invoice in front of his face. "What's up with this large order of pork spleens?"

The aggressive nature of my question threw him. He looked away for a few seconds. He then stepped back, waving me off, as if dismissing the importance of the matter.

I wouldn't let up. "What the hell are you trying to do?" I yelled.

"Just trying to make a little money for us," he said.

"Make a little money? No! You're just trying to increase the buyout. And while you're doing that, you could put both of us in jail."

He shrugged. "Who's gonna know?"

"I'm gonna know. And that's what's important. If I'm buying you out, it's my ass that's on the line if Topps gets investigated. So if you want this deal to go through, you better not pull any of this shit again." I stormed away to the office.

I spoke to the controller. "Don't pay this invoice. I'm handling it," I said.

He read the anger in my voice, looked up at me from his desk, and flashed a playful salute and a wink. "Aye, aye, captain," he said.

I called the district meat supervisor at the United States Department of Agriculture to inform him that we had a rogue order that we wanted to return to the supplier. I requested and received a product registration label to facilitate the return and at the same time served notice to the department that we were not using the product.

I called the broker that had sold the pork spleens to Topps. "We're shipping your order of pork spleens back to you," I said.

"Whaddya mean, 'shipping back to me?' You ordered the product; you have to pay for it."

"Not going to happen. This entire order is leaving our warehouse in the morning."

A long pause.

"Listen, Sachs," he said pointedly. "You're going to keep the order, and you're going to pay that invoice in full. I'm sending a guy over there tomorrow to pick up the money."

"You send a guy over here at his own risk, and I promise, he will not be returning with any of my money."

"You don't know who you're dealing with, Sachs. When Lew

Wassserman shows up, you better be ready to pay that invoice," he said as he slammed down the phone.

Lew Wasserman? I knew the name—an enforcer who was part of the Jewish Mafia that was connected to one of the five Mob families in New York. Wasserman was known to rough up guys who reneged on their loan payments.

The next day a large man—six foot three inches and weighing nearly three hundred pounds—walked into the Topps office. He identified himself as Lew Wasserman, asked to see my father, and was escorted to his desk.

My secretary, Theresa, came up to my office on the second floor a few minutes later. She appeared very distressed. "Steve," she said. "There's a large man downstairs at your father's desk, and he's threatening him."

I stood up. "You know, Theresa, it's really warm in here. I'm going to open a window before you send him up to see me."

Theresa's mouth dropped open. She then flashed a knowing look. "Oh, no," she said. "You're not going to do what I think you're going to do, are you?"

I smiled. "Why not? Nobody comes in here and threatens us. Tell that guy that I'll take care of the invoice. Just send him up here."

Theresa turned and left my office.

Within a few minutes Lew Wasserman was standing in the doorway to my office. "You the guy that's gonna settle this invoice?"

"Yes. Here's how we're going to settle it. You're going to have two trucks here tomorrow morning to pick up eight hundred boxes of pork spleens. If you don't send those trucks here, I'm going to have my guys put the boxes of pork spleens on the street to defrost."

Wasserman stepped closer to me. "If you don't pay me now,

you're gonna have a hard time walking tomorrow morning, let alone carrying boxes of pork spleens to the sidewalk."

"Sorry, pal. Not happening."

Wasserman said nothing. He stared at me for a few seconds—a death stare. Suddenly he made a clumsy bull rush toward me, leaning his mammoth frame forward and reaching toward my neck with his huge hands.

But he was no match for my quickness.

In an instant I stepped aside and forcibly used my left hand to grab his left shoulder and my right hand to push down on the back of his ass.

Totally off balance, he stumbled forward as the strength of my grip forced him toward the open window. I pushed him halfway out the window so that his head faced the street below and his arms dangled helplessly in front of him.

With one decisive move, I immobilized him by slamming the window down below his shoulders.

He screamed and flailed his arms in an aimless manner as he tried to find some leverage to push himself backwards to safety. It was no use.

I had him pinned in position by the window frame that by this time had made an indentation across his back. His neck bulged and his face became red with anger as he continued screaming for me to let him go.

"Whaddya say, Lew?" I yelled through the closed window. "You gonna have those trucks here tomorrow to take the boxes away?"

Finally, he gave in. "Yes ... yes!" he cried.

I opened the window, grabbed him by the shoulders, and pulled him back into my office. He landed on the floor with a thud, rolled over, and stared up at me with a startled look, trying to process what had happened. He crawled up on his knees and leaned on a chair to help himself get back on his feet. He said nothing but never took his eyes off me. He brushed off his clothes and left the building.

The next morning two refrigerated trucks pulled up to our warehouse. A crew of three men loaded the boxes of pork spleens into the trucks and drove away without saying a word to me.

As the trucks turned the corner, I tore up the invoice and threw it into a trash bin. I never heard from Lew Wasserman again. There were no repercussions from the Mob.

Six months later I finalized the deal to buy out my father, who retired and moved to Florida.

CHAPTER **20**

The Ham Caper Foiled

IT WAS PEACEFUL for a while on 9th Avenue, and Christmas was just around the corner. Two weeks before the holiday in 1984, my Topps crew and I were working overtime on a Saturday morning. On these extra workdays, I always bought coffee, rolls, and pastries for my crew. At 7:30 I left my store and walked over to Manganero's on the corner of 38th Street and 9th Avenue.

A light snow had begun to fall.

As I approached the corner, I heard a loud crash of shattering glass.

I walked to the corner and looked down the street to the area where the sound had come from. A huge Black man, approximately six feet, six inches tall, stood in front of a large broken window in Esposito's Pork Store.

Shattered glass littered the entire sidewalk.

The man wore thick, black construction-style boots and seemed undaunted by the glass all around his feet as he reached through the broken window.

I knew that Esposito's featured Smithfield Hams at Christmastime and had them hanging on hooks in the main display window. The huge man busily removed the large hams from the hooks and attached them to a thick belt underneath his raincoat. He worked fast. Not a wasted movement. More like a sleight-of-hand magician performing a trick. Within seconds he had slipped the string loops of five hams onto his belt, closed his raincoat, and began walking nonchalantly up 9th Avenue toward the Port Authority.

I assumed he planned to take a train or bus from the Port Authority to either Brooklyn or Harlem, where he could sell the hams to people preparing for their Christmas dinners. I followed him by walking on the opposite side of the street. I looked for a cop. Not one in sight on either side of the street.

I continued following him and crossed the street as he walked into the Port Authority Building. In a near sprint, I dashed into the main lobby and caught sight of him as he rode the escalator to the upstairs platforms. I walked up on the escalator, pushing myself past a few standing riders so I could close the gap between the ham thief and me.

A large crowd of people had gathered in the upstairs lobby waiting for an announcement of the platform for their departing train or bus.

I looked to my left and saw a Port Authority holding pen in the corner of the lobby, but no cops were stationed there. I knew I couldn't let this guy get off the escalator, blend into the crowd, and disappear while I searched for a Port Authority police officer. I needed to take action without delay. I stepped up closer to him, practically breathing down his neck.

Just as he began to step off the escalator, I jumped on his back and drove him down to the floor.

He was stunned, but his size and strength allowed him to roll over and try to push me away.

A clumsy wrestling match ensued as I tried to restrain him in the midst of other people who stumbled off the escalator in an awkward manner as they tried to avoid us.

He briefly broke away from my grasp, but I dove forward, grabbed him by the leg, and brought him down to the floor a second time.

He swung at me, but he got nothing but air. I swung and caught him flush on the left side of his face. He reeled onto his back. Hams came rolling out from underneath his raincoat.

Some people in the crowd screamed. Others laughed.

Within seconds the Port Authority police showed up and grabbed both of us. One of the cops picked up the hams.

As the cops dragged us away, I heard one of them—an older cop, probably a captain—asking for witnesses to come forward and tell him what happened.

I turned to see how many volunteered. More than a dozen people stepped up to provide their account of the brawl, but I was soon out of earshot and could not hear any of their statements.

The ham thief and I were taken down a hallway and summarily shoved into separate holding cells.

A half an hour passed.

The door to my holding cell opened. The captain walked in, accompanied by a younger cop who held a notepad and a pen.

"You wanna tell us why you jumped this guy?" he asked.

"He smashed the front window at Esposito's Pork Store on 9th and 38th and stole some hams from the display case. I followed him down here."

"Why didn't you call a cop?"

"Couldn't find one."

"So … you usually take the law into your own hands like this?"

"I couldn't let him get away."

He let out a grunt and turned to the younger officer. "Call that pork store and get Mr. Esposito down here right away. We need a statement from him."

"Right," said the young officer.

The captain looked at me with a smirk. "And tell him we won't let this guy out of here until he positively identifies his hams."

An hour later Esposito arrived and verified my story about the damage to his store and the robbery of the hams. The ham thief was booked for breaking and entering, property damage, and petty theft. Turns out he was a three-time loser and ended up doing some time in jail.

On Christmas Eve, Esposito rang our doorbell and presented a cooked, ten-pound ham to my wife.

It was delicious.

CHAPTER 21

New Orleans

Part 1

IN 1986 TOPPS, my meat packing business, was doing very well, and I had been in conversations to become partners with Joey D'urso. The future for our operation had a promising upside, and we needed more space to let it expand. We decided to move Topps into a newly renovated plant in New Jersey—one of the best business decisions I ever made.

Despite the distance from Brooklyn, my relationship with the Mob remained as strong as ever. I was not a member, but I was a respected associate of the "family." Mob members trusted me, and in return, I trusted them and always offered to help in any small way that I could.

Topps had become a national company and, as a result, I had to do quite a bit of traveling. On one occasion I had to travel to New Orleans to meet with two prospective customers. It had the potential of being a big deal, so I rescheduled my other commitments and booked a flight that departed within a few days.

Two days before I was scheduled to leave, I received a phone call from Sonny P. "Hey, Steve," he said. "Heard you're heading to New Orleans."

I hesitated for a second and then asked, "Sonny, how the hell did you know I was going to New Orleans?"

He laughed. "Stevie, you should know by now that we know everything. Information has a way of traveling to us."

I smiled. I thought to myself that he must have heard from Freddie Ruffino. Freddie was working for me at that time as the sales manager of my New York City distribution network. He had been associated with Charlie Anselmo and his crew as well as Sonny P from Brooklyn.

"What do you need in New Orleans?" I asked.

"Uncle John will explain it. I'll pick you up in the morning."

Uncle John's full name was John Faraci, but no one ever called him by his true last name. To his cronies in the Mob he was known simply as Johnny Green. He was given that moniker because he received, handled, and invested a lot of the Mob's money.

The Mob leaders were smart: they knew that the Feds were watching them and that someday the hammer might come down on their illegal sources of income. So Johnny Green's job was to find legal investment opportunities to provide a future money stream for the Mob and its families.

In the hierarchy of the Bonanno family, Johnny Green ranked either number three or number four, a lofty, powerful position for sure and an inarguable indication of his importance to the Mob.

Those of us of the younger generation shared a special relationship with the man and were privileged to refer to him as Uncle John. If he asked for a favor, I always tried to oblige, as long as it was not illegal. Once the favor was delivered, he made sure we were compensated—not necessarily in money, but often in terms of a future favor in return.

A "saved" favor from Uncle John was worth a lot—certainly more than a few hundred dollars in your wallet. Besides, I preferred to be owed a favor than to owe one to the Mob.

Despite the power he wielded within the Mob hierarchy, Uncle John never pressured me to do a favor for him. He understood and respected my commitment to run a legitimate business and not get involved in any illegal activity. But he also respected and appreciated that any favor I did for him would be kept strictly confidential.

I had been introduced to Uncle John years earlier through my friendship with Freddie Ruffino and Charlie Anselmo. Uncle John was a short man—only about five feet, five inches tall—with a trim build and a balding head. But what stood out the most about his appearance was the ever-present smile on his face. He was a pleasant, happy person who always made me feel welcome to be in his company.

I never took Uncle John's diminutive stature and warm, smiling countenance for granted. I respected his reputation as a major figure in the Mob and quickly realized that his prerequisite for respect in return was truthfulness in all interpersonal dealings. As a result, I never even remotely considered lying to him about any question he asked or denying him a favor that he sought from me.

Uncle John was a modest man who never bragged about his position of power or personal accomplishments. In fact, it wasn't until much later in my life that I learned from another source that he had landed on Normandy beach on D-Day in 1944 and was awarded a Bronze Star for meritorious service.

Although some members of the New York Mob were involved in the lucrative business of dealing drugs, Uncle John stayed clear of this activity for his entire career. He was also aware of my passion to keep drugs off the streets near the schools in my neighborhood and never interfered or discouraged my efforts, which was one of the many reasons for which he earned my utmost respect.

Over time our relationship grew very close and I looked upon him as a benevolent uncle who was looking out for my best interests. I believed he enjoyed taking young, ambitious people under his wing and watching them become highly successful. I loved Uncle John and felt honored to help him in any way that I could. I never asked to be paid for any favor I did for him, nor did he ever offer a financial reward.

And perhaps more importantly, I never discussed my conversations with Uncle John with anyone, which was a basic foundation of our mutually respectful relationship. Nevertheless, he had his own special way of keeping track of the balance sheet and always found a way to take care of me in some way down the road.

The next morning Sonny P picked me up and we drove to Brooklyn. He dropped me off at Loehmann's Plaza off Coney Island Avenue. "Go into that Burger King and have a cup of coffee," he said.

I didn't question him. I got out of the car, walked inside, ordered a cup of black coffee, and sat down at a small booth.

Twenty minutes later a big guy wearing black pants, a black crewneck sweater, and a black jacket walked in and looked around for a few seconds. He came over and sat down next to me.

I had never seen the guy before. I looked at him and nodded, knowing full well what was coming next.

"Let's go," he said. "John is waiting for you."

He drove me to a plumbing shop along the New Utrecht El, saying nothing along the way, but I didn't expect much conversation. I knew that the details in these matters always came from the top, and no one, least of all a driver, ever wanted to be accused of overstepping their bounds by speaking for the boss or unwittingly offering incorrect information to someone.

I got out of the car and followed the driver as he led me through the plumbing shop. I passed all the young wannabees who were hanging around drinking cappuccino espresso while waiting for orders to go out and collect money from some bookie or a business or to deliver a message to other associates.

The driver stopped by a doorway to an open area in the back of the shop. "He's here," he said.

Suddenly a boisterous voice yelled from the back, "Stevie! Come on back! We have breakfast waiting for you."

I walked into the office and was greeted with a huge bear hug from Uncle John.

"Stevie! So good to see you. How's your business?" he asked.

"It's good, Uncle John. Growing bigger all the time."

"You're a hard worker. I'm not surprised. I'm very proud of you. I heard that you and Joey D. are going to be partners. Good move!" Then he pointed to a large rectangular table covered with platters of food and next to it, a smaller table with two chairs. "Sit down," he said. "Let's have something to eat."

I fully expected Italian-style cheeses, prosciutto, capicola, mortadella, and salami, along with an assortment of Italian bread and rolls. Instead Uncle John had bought lox, whitefish, bagels, cream cheese, and an assortment of rugelach cookies—a Zabar's special. No doubt he wanted his favorite Jewish boy to feel right at home.

We loaded our plates and sat down at the small table.

In between bites, he pushed his chair closer to me. "Stevie," he said. "I've got a problem in New Orleans, and I need you to check on something."

"Anything you need, Uncle John."

"Sonny P has a cousin in New Orleans. Runs a crawfish operation that's been very successful. Sonny P said he wanted to expand it. Might be a good deal for us to partner with this guy. So we invested two hundred fifty large in his business."

I knew that "two hundred fifty large" meant $250,000, so that number garnered my complete attention. In 1987 that was a lot of money.

He took another bite from his bagel and continued. "The guy called us a few weeks ago and said he had some bad news. A tornado hit his crawfish barge and wrecked his boon and netting. The fucking barge was destroyed. He was not insured. All of our investment is gone."

"That's a tough blow," I said, but I knew there must be more to this story.

"Yeah, but we're not so sure about this guy. I want you to pay a visit to him and make sure he's telling us the truth."

"No problem. I happen to be leaving tomorrow."

"I'll make all the arrangements with our people down there to pick you up at the airport and get you a nice place to stay. We'll provide all of your transportation."

"No problem."

"Look," he said. "I need you to find out whatever you can about this guy's operation, get some pictures of the destroyed barge, and see me when you get back."

Nothing else had to be said. I understood my assignment, and no further clarification was necessary.

We finished eating while talking about families, baseball, and a bit of politics.

Looking back on the times I spent with Uncle John, I realize that I relished those moments. He was a true gentleman. To this day I can say that I still miss him.

When I got on the plane for New Orleans the next morning, though, I had a very uneasy feeling about the assignment.

I had no idea what to expect.

CHAPTER 22

New Orleans

Part 2

I WAS ALWAYS amazed at how far into society the tentacles of the Mob reached. Members left no stone unturned when it came to developing and maintaining connections. They had contacts and financial interests everywhere, within all areas of commerce and transportation, unions, the garment industry, the hotel industry, the public and private educational system, the Catholic Church, and yes, even the police. This last point was rather dramatically emphasized after I landed in New Orleans and walked to baggage claim. I waited until my suitcase slid down the carousel, lifted it off, and put it down on the floor. I looked around for a few minutes, but no one approached me.

Gradually, all the passengers retrieved their luggage and walked away from the carousel.

I stood alone waiting for someone—my unknown escort—to walk over, signal with a wave, or call my name.

But nothing.

I noticed a tall police officer leaning against a pillar, seemingly disinterested in the nearly quiet baggage claim area.

Suddenly he stood up straight. His eyes focused on me, and he began taking quick steps in my direction.

My first thought was that I had been bagged—the victim of a tip-off by someone who knew I was involved with the Mob. I swallowed hard but stood firm as he approached.

Am I about to be taken into custody? I thought.

He leaned in toward me. "Excuse me, sir," he said. "Are you Steve?"

I looked up at him, almost stunned that he knew my name. "Yes, I am," I said.

He moved closer so that our conversation would be a bit more private. He had an odd look, almost like the goofy cop in *Smokey and the Bandit*.

"I'm from the sheriff's office, and I'm here to provide your transportation today."

My transportation? In New Orleans, did the police provide taxicab service? The answer is "yes," if they received a request from the Mob.

On the drive to my destination, I sat in the back seat of the police cruiser. In between the two front seats, a shotgun rested on the console, the barrel of which was pointed directly at me.

"You need to pull over," I said.

The deputy looked surprised, almost taken aback by my sharp command. "Something wrong?" he asked.

"Yeah, your fuckin' shotgun is pointed right at me, and I don't want to be collateral damage when you drive over some bump in the road."

The deputy waved his hand in acknowledgment of my request. He pulled the cruiser into the breakdown lane, and I got into the front passenger seat.

After a short ride we arrived at police headquarters, where I received a huge greeting from Les Bonnano, a member of the

Bonanno family, and the sheriff himself.

Les had to leave Brooklyn years earlier when he "messed up" a made-man of another Mob family. In the unwritten code of the Mob, his was a sin for which one usually paid with his life. But the Bonnanos negotiated with the other family to determine Les's fate. In exchange for some major territorial concessions, Les was spared but had to be moved out of town. So he was relocated to New Orleans, where he had become a special assistant to the sheriff.

In addition to his primary duties with the sheriff's office, Les ran a game-machine business for his former cronies in Brooklyn. On top of that, Les and the sheriff formed a partnership to run a boxing operation utilizing prisoners in the county jail as the primary source of boxing talent. The operation offered the prisoners free training from certified boxing trainers. Then the best boxers were eligible to fight matches in Mississippi. All the winning prize money, of course, was funneled to the Mob. The prisoners were just happy to have a few days of supervised parole as well as the promise of some perks when they returned to their cells. Occasionally one of their best fighters qualified for a major boxing program in Atlantic City. When this happened, Joey D and I often got front row seats next to some of the Mafia kingpins.

The sheriff took me on a tour of police headquarters and proudly showed a room in the back of the building, his personal office suite. Beyond plush was the only fitting term to describe it. I guessed that neither the taxpayers nor newspaper reporters ever got a glimpse of that suite.

After the tour the sheriff called out to his goofy deputy, "Take Steve over to the Royal Sonesta on Bourbon Street. Check him in for a suite."

Since the goofy deputy's shotgun was still in his cruiser, I took no chances and sat in the front passenger seat again. We arrived at the hotel after a short ride and walked across the lobby to Guest Registration.

"Checking in Mr. Sachs for a suite. He's the guest of the New Orleans Sheriff's Department," the deputy said.

"I'm terribly sorry," said the clerk, "but there are no suites available. There are a couple of conventions in town, and rooms are hard to come by."

I told the deputy to get on the phone with Les to see what he wanted me to do. Within ten minutes the sheriff arrived at the hotel and walked up to the registration desk. "Let me see your list of registrants for the suites," he demanded. He ran his finger over the list of names, paused as he picked one out, and looked up at the clerk. "Ring up suite two zero zero five," he barked.

The clerk dutifully obeyed, and after a few seconds handed the phone to the sheriff.

"This is Sheriff Foti. Pack up your belongings and vacate your fuckin' room within the next fifteen minutes." The sheriff handed the phone back to the clerk, pointed to two chairs in the lobby, and motioned to me to take a seat.

I sat down and leaned back in one of the chairs, thoroughly enjoying the scene that was playing right in front of me.

Sure enough, within a few minutes, an older, disheveled man arrived at the front desk pulling his luggage and mumbling to himself. His shirt was partially untucked, his hair was uncombed, and he looked as if he had just rolled out of bed. The man glanced briefly at the sheriff sitting next to me, but quickly diverted his attention to the clerk at the desk. He signed his checkout statement without saying a word and then walked out the front door looking straight ahead, obviously avoiding any eye contact with the sheriff.

The sheriff stared at the man as the uncomfortable scene

played out but said nothing until the older man had left the hotel. Then he turned to me. "Don't feel bad for that bastard. He just got released from the county jail where he was serving time for some white-collar crime. He embezzled money from the local Catholic dioceses. Felons like him don't deserve any sympathy, let alone to stay in a fancy place like this."

I just nodded, never expressing my thoughts, but I knew that in his own hypocritical way, the sheriff was conveniently ignoring his own corruption.

Les arrived and joined the sheriff and me for a drink at the bar.

"Around six o'clock you're gonna be picked up by a guy named Bobby. He's gonna take you to dinner and then show you what happened to his crawfish operation. What's it all about?" asked Les.

I didn't know how much Uncle John had told Les about this matter, so I decided to play it cool. "You know, Johnny Green makes some investments here and there. I'm just here to collect some information for him."

Les apparently bought my explanation and shrugged. He ordered another drink from the bartender and asked no other questions about my dinner meeting.

By mid-afternoon, Les and the sheriff had departed and I was firmly ensconced in my luxurious suite that had every amenity a guest could desire: two television sets, a well-stocked refrigerator filled with snacks, an assortment of liquors and other alcoholic beverages, etc. I relaxed on the bed watching television, but my mind kept drifting to the upcoming meeting with the man whose destroyed crawfish business had cost the Mob a large chunk of money, $250 large.

Serious money.

If this guy's story of an unfortunate act of nature was not the truth, I had no choice but to inform Uncle John of the facts. My report, therefore, could result in dire consequences, so dire that this guy's life could be on the line. Simply stated, you just didn't double-cross the Mob without paying a severe penalty.

Around five p.m. the phone in my room rang and I was informed that my guest had arrived and was waiting in the lobby. I walked out of the elevator and was greeted by a smiling face on a medium-sized guy about five feet, nine inches tall.

"Hey, Steve. I'm Bobby. Thanks for coming down."

We shook hands and I returned a cordial smile, all the while noticing that his hand was soft and supple, hardly that of a man who worked in a labor-intensive, physically demanding business such as the crawfish industry.

"Come on, Steve," he said. "I'm taking you to a great restaurant not far from the river. You'll love the food, and then later I can take you out to see the destroyed barge. It was a terrible tragedy and a huge loss."

After a short ride we arrived at a large restaurant in a busy section of New Orleans. We sat down at a table for two and over the next hour and a half feasted on an assortment of terrific food. Bobby kept ordering more wine for our table; I drank cautiously, trying to stay alert for our impending visit to the barge. Bobby, however, seemed perfectly content to spend a leisurely time in the restaurant.

I sensed he was stalling. I refused another glass of wine and instead ordered a cup of cappuccino to finish off the dining extravaganza.

The sun was beginning to set.

"Hey, Bobby," I said. "I've really enjoyed the drinks and dinner, but I need to see the barge while there's still enough daylight to inspect the damage."

"Oh, yes, of course. Sorry. Guess I just lost track of the time."

In the car he appeared to be a bit nervous, glancing around, almost unsure of the direction we were heading. "How's my cousin, Sonny P, doin'?" he asked.

"Sonny P's just fine," I said, not wanting to engage in too much discussion that might distract him from the main objective of getting to the damaged barge.

"That's great. And while I'm thinking of it, be sure to tell the guys in New York how much I appreciated their investment in my business. I feel terrible that things turned out this way."

"Don't worry, I'll pass along your sentiments."

"Thanks," he said. "Yeah, I never expected this."

I didn't reply.

We drove a short distance to a bank of the Mississippi River and got out of his car. He pointed to a large barge that was capsized and resting about fifty yards offshore.

"That tornado was devastating," he said. "We lost everything. The engine was destroyed, the traps smashed to bits, and all of our equipment and supplies on board were ruined. See how the netting is ripped and the boom is split in half? Nothing could be salvaged... a total loss. And I still have to pay to get this rig towed out of the water and scrapped."

I said nothing. My eyes were focused on the moss and barnacles on the sides of the capsized barge that was halfway under water. For a barge that was supposedly destroyed less than three months earlier, the exterior indicated that the level of crud and deterioration was more likely a result of sitting in the water for years, rather than months. I wasn't buying his story.

"Mind if I take a few pictures to show your partners in New York?"

"No, not at all," he said. "Take as many as you need."

After I took a few pictures, we got back into his car and drove away from the river.

"How about another cup of cappuccino?" he asked.

"Sure," I said. I said little else as I looked idly out the window, trying to process the scene of that decrepit barge resting offshore.

Bobby seemed a bit edgy and kept glancing over at me, seemingly unnerved by my silence. "Let me take you to my family's restaurant," he said. "It's a great place."

"It's all right with me, if they have great cappuccino."

We drove to the outskirts of the Tulane University campus. He parked the car and we walked about a block to a fabulous-looking upscale restaurant and lounge complete with walk-up stations to order food. The décor had an Italian theme and was beautifully decorated.

Even though it was a mid-week evening, the restaurant was a bustling, noisy place, every table filled with diners—families, college kids, couples, both young and old, and business men in ties and jackets.

As we walked in, Bobby received a royal welcome from every employee in the place. He introduced me to his mother at the pasta station, his father at the cappuccino espresso station, and his sister at the pastry station. A guitarist in the lounge played some upbeat music while the lively patrons consumed beer and wine.

He escorted me to a small table for two that had just been prepared for us.

"Looks like you've got a popular place here," I said.

"Yes, we opened about six months ago, and it has really taken off."

"You said it's your family's business?"

He hesitated for a second. "Well, I'm the principal owner, but as you can see, my whole family is involved here."

I offered a congratulatory smile and nodded as a waitress

brought over our cappuccinos. As I took my first sip, I continued to look around, taking in the entire scene of the apparent
money-making enterprise. I knew almost instantly that I had discovered what happened to Uncle John's 250 large. Rather than
sinking into the Mississippi, the Mob's investment was thriving
right there in front of me. I finished my cup of cappuccino and
begged off from Bobby's offer of another round of drinks. There
was little or no conversation at our table. I found no need to ask
any more questions.

In a short while I contacted Les, who had agreed to pick
me up. On the way back to my hotel, we stopped at Michelle's
Tavern—one of his favorite bars—for a night cap.

While we were having a drink, he introduced me to the
woman who owned the tavern. She was a little older, but very
sexy and flirtatious.

"Can you dance Cajun style?" she asked.

"No, but I'm willing to let you teach me," I said.

The DJ began playing a haunting, romantic song. We got on
the dance floor. Almost immediately she pushed her body close
to mine and led me in a series of sensuous and rhythmic moves.
I had no doubt that she was delivering a definite signal. More
likely, an invitation.

Many of the patrons at the bar had their eyes on us.

The music eventually stopped. Arm in arm we walked over
to the bar, where Les had been enjoying our "show" on the
dance floor. He looked at me and couldn't contain his laughter.
"Sorry, sweetie," he said to the woman. "This guy has an early
morning meeting. I've got to take him back to his hotel."

We finished our drinks, and I told her I'd be back in a couple
of months.

Les and I headed out to the parking lot.

Les continued laughing all the way to the car.

"What's so funny?" I asked.

"How old do you think that broad is?"

"I don't know, maybe fifty?"

"She's over seventy, you idiot. She's old enough to be your grandmother."

I then joined in the laughter.

In fact, we laughed all the way to the hotel.

We exchanged a few more stories and said our goodbyes when he dropped me off.

As I walked up to my hotel room, reality sank in. I was in possession of some very serious information about a man who had apparently tried to scam the Mob.

How was I going to explain it to Uncle John?

CHAPTER 23

New Orleans

Part 3

THE NEXT DAY I met with my prospective client and cemented a nice new deal for my business—two supermarket chains in New Orleans. Things were definitely on the upswing for Topps, and it seemed like we were on our way to be a major player on the national scene of the meat packing and distribution industry.

As I boarded the plane for my flight back to New York, I was feeling good about my new contract, but not so good about the news I had to deliver to Uncle John. How would Uncle John take it, knowing that this guy in New Orleans had scammed him out of 250 large? Worse yet, the guy playing the scam was a close relative of a Mob associate. And speaking of whom, what did Sonny P know about the scam?

I knew Sonny P wasn't in on the deal, but had he been taken in by his cousin's lies? Would he become an innocent victim in this mess merely by his association with his cousin?

I tried to put these thoughts out of my mind and catch some sleep on the flight, but nothing worked. All I could think of was the best way to deliver my report to Uncle John.

After we landed, I took the escalator downstairs to baggage claim. Not surprisingly, Sonny P was waiting for me. He flashed an uneasy smile and asked, "How did things go?"

"Not here," I said. "We'll talk in the car."

"Sure," he said as he looked away, somewhat taken aback by my curt response. Then he shrugged as if the delay didn't matter. When he looked back at me, he caught my deadly stare and quickly turned his head toward the luggage as it slowly passed by on the carousel.

No other words were spoken.

On the ride from the airport to drop me off at my house, I waited for Sonny P to start the conversation. Finally, he asked, "Okay, Stevie, I've gotta tell ya', I'm worried about my cousin. What happened down there? Is he in trouble with Uncle John?"

"You mean your cousin who just outfitted his brand-new restaurant with Uncle John's money? The same cousin who made up a bullshit story that his crawfish barge was destroyed in a tornado?"

"Oh, shit! I had no idea! Don't tell me he tried to pull something over on them."

"It looks like he did, Sonny. And this situation is gonna get ugly fast."

"Stevie," he said, as he raised his voice, almost begging, "he must have gotten himself into some kind of a jam. Maybe the original deal didn't work out. I'll talk to him and make sure he pays the money back from the restaurant profits."

I looked at Sonny P and then stared straight ahead. I didn't reply.

A few minutes passed.

Finally, Sonny P turned toward me and asked, "So what are you going to say to Uncle John?"

"I've got to tell him the truth."

"C'mon, Stevie, if you tell him the truth, my cousin is history."

"And if I lie to Uncle John, one of these days you and I will be asked to attend a meeting at the plumbing shop, and we'll both get whacked before the meeting is over. They'll bury our bodies somewhere, and our families will never know what happened to us."

Sonny P looked away and kept driving, obviously trying to process my dire analysis. He rubbed his right hand through his hair and shook his head. Sonny P was in obvious emotional turmoil. Perhaps he was scared to death about Uncle John's perception of his involvement in his cousin's scam. "How the fuck did this happen to me? I never should have listened to him in the first place," he said.

I said nothing. There was no use in adding to Sonny P's despair.

A few minutes passed.

"So…what are you going to do, Stevie?" he asked.

"I'm going to tell him exactly what I saw in New Orleans. No sugar coating; just the truth."

"And what about me?"

"That's between you and Uncle John. My report has nothing to do with you."

"What do you think I should say after you talk to him?"

"My advice is to just tell him you're sorry you recommended your cousin to him and you're especially sorry that your cousin misled him. This is on your cousin, not you. Then ask Uncle John to give your cousin a chance to make amends."

There was no further conversation. Sonny P pulled the car up to the curb in front of my house.

I grabbed my suitcase and slammed the trunk closed.

He drove away.

As his car disappeared into a stream of rear taillights, I wondered if Sonny P would be lucky enough to survive this mess.

CHAPTER **24**

New Orleans

Part 4

TWO DAYS LATER I received my instructions to drive to a local Dunkin' Donuts and sit at a booth inside and wait for a pickup. I sat in the booth drinking a cup of coffee and watching the morning crowd queuing up to get its caffeine fix on the way to work.

A different guy than my last pickup, this time in work clothes—jeans and a dark blue sweatshirt—ordered a large coffee, paid for it, and then turned to walk out the door. As he walked past, he gave a quick glance toward me and an almost imperceptible nod.

I knew he must be my ride. I waited for a few seconds, grabbed my coffee, got up from the booth, and followed him out the door.

He walked briskly to a black Lincoln, opened the driver's side door, and got into the car. As he sat down, he looked back at me and gave a signal with his head for me to get into the front passenger seat.

On the ride to the plumbing shop, the guy did not say a

word. He was all business; no small talk whatsoever.

I had a feeling that Uncle John's entire crew knew that something was up, and I was right in the middle of it.

Once we arrived at the plumbing shop, I was escorted to the back area, where Uncle John greeted me with his usual big smile and a huge hug. "Stevie! How was your trip?" he asked as he motioned to the driver to leave us alone and slowly closed the door. "Come. Come. Sit down," he said. "Sit down so we can talk."

I tossed my jacket on a side table and sat down.

He pulled a chair up close to me, sat down, and leaned forward. "I heard you closed two nice deals for yourself in New Orleans."

"Yes, I did."

Then I paused. "How did you know?" I asked. "I haven't said much about the new contracts since I got home."

He looked at me with the usual twinkle in his eyes. "Oh, you know, Stevie, word has a way of getting back to us." He laughed a little and continued. "A guy from New Orleans called me. He's an associate of the family down there. He said he expects a seven percent brokerage fee on your new deal."

"But I negotiated this deal on my own," I said. "Nobody intervened on the terms of this deal."

"I know. Don't worry. I told him, 'No brokerage fee.' You're all set. That guy will never bother you."

His words "That guy will never bother you" meant that Uncle John had warned the Mob associate to leave me alone or else face dire consequences.

"Thank you," I said.

He waved off my comment and pivoted to the main reason for my visit. "So...tell me," he said. "Did you meet this guy, Bobby, Sonny P's cousin in New Orleans?"

"Yes, I did. I spent a few hours with him on the night I arrived."

"And what did he have to say?"

"He told me the same story that he told you—a tornado blew through that section of New Orleans and destroyed his barge and all of his equipment. There was so much damage that he had to suspend his crawfish operation."

Uncle John nodded but followed up quickly with the critical question. "Did you see this destroyed barge?"

"Yes. He drove me down to the Mississippi River where we could see a capsized barge about fifty yards offshore..." I paused, trying to think of just the right words to break the news to him.

He picked up on my hesitation.

"And ... what did you think of this barge?"

"Before I met up with him, I checked with the front desk clerk at my hotel about the date of the storm. The tornado blew through there only three months ago, but the barge was covered with so many barnacles and so much mold that it must have been there for years."

He pursed his lips and furrowed his brow as he looked down, processing my statement for a few seconds. He looked up at me. "So this guy's story is bullshit?"

"Yes. Totally bullshit. I don't think he ever had a crawfish operation."

"So where's my money?"

"Later that night he took me to a fancy restaurant—a gastronomic galleria—a brand new, upscale place. Right near Tulane University. Walk-up food stations for pasta, salads, entrees, and desserts. Cappuccino espresso ... the whole works. The place was packed with college students and businessmen. A real popular place. Seems like his whole family works there—his mother, father, sister ... maybe others I didn't meet."

"He owns this place?"

"Yes."

He paused again, lifted his left arm to the armrest of his chair, and leaned his head on his hand as he lightly rubbed his index finger back and forth across his upper lip. He appeared deep in thought. "Do you think Sonny P knew about all of this?" he asked.

"No, Uncle John. Sonny P had no idea. His cousin never told him a thing about the restaurant."

He stared off again for a few seconds, obviously analyzing all this information.

I had no intentions of interrupting him and waited quietly.

Finally, he sat up and said, "So this guy bankrolled his fancy restaurant with my two-fifty large?"

"Looks that way to me, Uncle John. I don't see any other possibility."

We spent the next few minutes looking at the pictures I had taken of the decrepit barge. Uncle John examined them closely and then tossed them on the table in apparent disgust.

I could tell he was fuming inside but didn't want to say very much or show me the depth of his anger. If you dared to double-cross a Mob member—especially by trying to swindle him out of his money—you usually paid with your life. But he would never tell you his specific plans to rub someone out.

The Mob never took the chance that you could become a government witness and testify against a member in a murder trial. No, those discussions were confined to a very close-knit circle.

Above all, I knew it was not my place to ask Uncle John what he planned to do. In fact, none of my friends in the Mob ever told me directly about any of the crimes they carried out, which was an essential part of our relationship and the main reason it was so successful for so many years. They didn't tell, and I didn't ask.

Uncle John stood up from his chair, signaling that our brief meeting was over. "Stevie, you did a huge favor for me. Thank you," he said. He led me to the door, opened it, and waved for the driver to take me back to the Dunkin' Donuts to pick up my car.

On the ride back I thought of all the possible outcomes for the New Orleans problem. None of them were good.

Sonny P's cousin might have an untimely "accident" in which both legs would be broken, or he might suddenly disappear, never to be seen again.

But in this case, I knew that Uncle John's objective was not simply vengeance. Rather, his first priority was to get his money back and turn this loss into a profit.

I didn't hear much for a couple of weeks, but gradually the story leaked out to all of us who were connected to the family.

The Mob sent a lawyer and two tough guys to New Orleans for a meeting with Bobby. They presented a contract to him in which the Mob legally took control of the Gastro-Galleria restaurant. Under the terms of this contract, profits would be divided on a two-thirds/one-third basis with the larger portion going to the Mob.

At first Bobby refused to sign the deal, but then one of the tough guys grabbed him by the neck and squeezed it so hard that Bobby's face turned blue. The other tough guy shoved his head down, held it over the contract, and forced Bobby to read every word out loud to verify that he understood all the terms before he placed his signature at the bottom.

Bobby cried and begged for his life.

The lawyer sat by, quietly observing the scene and waiting

for the expected capitulation by the offending party.

When Bobby finally signed on the dotted line, the contract was soaked with the tears from his eyes and the perspiration that ran off his forehead.

I never heard another word about the New Orleans matter.

Uncle John never volunteered any information, and I never asked.

It was simply the Mob's way of extorting justice for such an egregious offense: trying to steal their money.

Sonny P didn't talk to me for two months, but in his heart, he knew that I had to tell Uncle John the truth. He also knew that I had spared him the embarrassment of not having to explain himself to Uncle John.

Eventually Sonny P and I were tight again.

When his mother passed away, he asked me to ride with him to the cemetery in the family limo—an honor bestowed only to one's closest friends.

CHAPTER 25

The Greek

IN 1986 JOEY D'urso and I continued our deep conversations about forming a partnership with my growing Topps hamburger business. The discussions were always quite animated.

"What do I know about selling hamburgers?" he asked.

"Look," I said. "We can renovate your old Empire Beef plant in Elizabeth and have lots of room to expand."

"Expand? I'm losing six grand a week. Guys like me are going down the tubes because we can't match the prices of the beef that's being shipped in from the West."

I knew all too well what Joey D was talking about. Local meat cutters couldn't compete with the big meat packers out West—Conagra and IBP—because they were cutting the beef and then using a new technology, Cryovac, to seal and preserve it before shipping the meat to buyers on the East Coast. The meat arrived in the East in only two days, fresh as the day it was cut, and the price was ten to fifteen cents less per pound than the best price that local meat cutters could offer.

I pushed hard for Joey D to see the upside of joining me. "Instead of trying to compete with those guys, we can be one of their customers, buy our meat from them and convert it into hamburger for less money than buying locally," I said.

"I feel bad for my relatives. If I become partners with you in the hamburger business and close the plant in Elizabeth for renovations, they're all gonna lose their jobs. What are they gonna do?"

"No problem. While we're doing the renovations to your plant, we'll train all of them in hamburger production. It's a win-win."

Joey thought for a second and then did a complete turn-around. "You're right. Let's do it."

Joey D's decision did not surprise me in the least, but what did surprise me was how much I benefitted from this business arrangement. He not only became my partner, but he also served as a lifelong confidant and a protective older brother. Joey D not only enhanced my business; he also enhanced my life.

Whenever a business deal was on the table, we talked things over, but in the end, he deferred to me for the final decision. If someone approached him with a distribution offer for Topps, his answer was always straightforward: "Talk to the Jew." Later, when he told me what he said, we'd laugh like hell.

Joey was an old-school guy. He didn't like or trust the stock market. Instead, he liked lending his money to restaurants and food enterprises at the going rate of eight to ten percent. He particularly liked lending money to Italian restaurants in New Jersey so he could stop by to collect his monthly payments and also enjoy some delicious Italian food.

Joey was the only Sicilian I ever met who didn't like garlic. He called in advance of the collection date and requested Italian gravy without garlic. And, of course, the debtor obliged.

At five feet, six inches tall and weighing nearly 280 pounds, Joey always professed to be on a diet, but when it came to delicious Italian food, he simply could not resist. Since I often accompanied him on his collection visits, I found that my weight was ballooning as well.

Our Topps business was growing, and we were growing right along with it.

Joey D was a great family man for whom I had tremendous admiration, almost jealousy. He had the love and respect of his entire family—children, nieces and nephews—because of the way he always cared for all of them. He made sure they had jobs and financial help in times of need. If there was a crisis, he was there. No questions asked; no excuses.

His mantra was quite simple: "What can I do to make this better?"

Except from my mother, I never enjoyed such appreciation and love from my family. As a result, I found myself jumping on Joey's bandwagon to do whatever I could to help his extended family through our new joint venture in Elizabeth, New Jersey.

Our initial game plan involved sending some of his relatives to my plant on 38th Street every three months for hands-on training. They grasped their education very quickly and showed me that they were good workers. Along the way I forged a great relationship with all of them.

When the Elizabeth renovation was completed, I hoped that both of Joey's sons—Joe Jr. and Anthony—could work with me in the new plant. They were terrific kids. But Joey was still operating his Demar chicken and pork operation and needed one of his sons to help him there.

One day I overheard his oldest son, Anthony, talking to Joey on the telephone. "I love this hamburger business, Dad," he said. "Steve is a great guy, but he is fucking crazy when it comes to dealin' with bad guys. If somebody crosses him or does something to this neighborhood, look out; they end up dealin' with Steve."

I knew right away that Anthony was a perfect fit to work with me.

The other relatives were divided equally between Topps and Demar. There were four Anthonys, two Johns, two Josephs, and a lot of other friends and relatives, all with ties of some sort to Joey D. We had a good mix; every one of them proved to be a loyal and hardworking employee.

While Anthony was working with me on 38th Street during his training period, he witnessed quite a few incidents on the street. This was the time when I was busily involved with the shenanigans of the drug pushers on 9th Avenue and 38th Street. However, another incident involved a character known as The Greek.

John "The Greek" was a chef at the Riverdale Diner but also had a side business through which he made and sold hamburgers to other diners, restaurants, and coffee shops in New York City and the Bronx. John bought his meat from Schuster Meats, owned by Bernie Schuster, in the famous 14th Street Meat Market. The Greek paid ten cents over the boneless beef wholesale price as listed on the daily printed wholesale price sheet.

One day John realized that Bernie had been fudging the price sheets and had been charging him thirteen cents over the wholesale price. John stopped doing business with Bernie Schuster immediately, called him a cheater, and refused to pay the balance due from previous orders—$15,000.

A bitter relationship ensued.

When John came over to do business with us at Topps, I had no idea of those previous issues and sold ready-made hamburgers to him. John complied by paying for his orders on time weekly.

One day Bernie Schuster parked across the street from my Topps plant and confronted John the Greek as he was picking up an order. "You owe me fifteen grand, you cheap bastard," Bernie yelled.

"You cheated me for two years. I owe you nothing," the Greek screamed back.

I heard the commotion and walked outside.

The two men stood face to face, pointing at each other and shouting at the top of their lungs.

I stepped between them and turned to speak directly to Bernie. "Take this argument away from my plant and don't come around here again to harass one of my customers," I said.

"He owes me fifteen grand," yelled Bernie. He leaned into me, trying to continue his rant against the Greek.

I pushed him away and issued a final warning to Bernie. "If he owes money to you, take him to Small Claims Court and sue him. But stay off my street!"

Bernie backed away, turned, and walked over to his car. Within minutes he drove away.

Two days later he came back and once again parked across from Topps.

I knew he must be waiting for the Greek to pick up another order, so I walked out and stared directly at him with my hands on my hips.

He started the engine and drove away.

I sensed that Bernie Schuster was not about to give up his vendetta quietly. I decided to make some inquiries with my friends in the Mob. I was told that Bernie had a hot temper, a "loose cannon" personality, and was known to carry a gun. My friends asked if I needed them to make a visit to Bernie, more or less an "intervention," to make him back off.

I thanked them for the offer but decided to deal with him myself.

The next day, at the same time of the morning, Bernie returned and parked his car in the same spot directly across from the front door of my plant.

I walked out the front door and never looked across the street at his car. Instead, I turned left and walked up to the corner of 38th Street and crossed over to the other side of the street. I slowly walked down the street and approached his car from behind. I walked up to the driver's side of the car and tapped on the window.

The tapping startled Bernie.

I motioned to him to roll down his window.

As the window rolled down, I reached into my pocket and pulled out a plastic replica of a .38 snub-nosed revolver and quickly stuffed it into his ear.

"Reach for the roof!" I said.

Bernie recoiled slightly and his eyes opened wide in fear. His mouth sagged open. He tried to speak, but no words came out. He reached up until his hands touched the roof of the car cabin. His body trembled.

I reached into his inside jacket pocket and slipped out a gun—a real .38 handgun. "Get the fuck out of here before I shoot a hole in your ear. And don't ever come back," I warned.

Bernie turned the ignition key and quietly drove away.

I thought that incident might be the end to the affair, but I was wrong.

Two days later Bernie showed up at my plant with two guys—his foreman, who stood at six feet, four inches tall and Bernie's son, who was also a big guy, about six feet, one inch tall.

When I saw them crossing the street, I immediately grabbed my bat—always kept nearby my desk for quick access—and met them outside my door.

The foreman stepped close to me. "I don't like it when someone threatens my boss," he said.

"I don't like it when someone harasses my customers," I responded.

He made a motion to swing at me.

But he was slow.

I was fast.

Within a heartbeat I rapped him in the knees with my bat.

He let out a painful scream and went down on the sidewalk. He looked up at me with fear in his eyes, rolled away, struggled to his feet, and limped toward the parked car.

Bernie and his son bolted toward their car without saying a word and without offering a helping hand to the wounded foreman.

The foreman crawled into the back seat. The car sped away as he closed the rear passenger door.

Two hours later I received a phone call. "Sachs?" the caller said.

'You've got him," I responded.

"This is Teddy Maggio."

I knew the name but had never met him. He had a meat business farther down on 14th Street and was known to be a guy well-connected to the Mob in Brooklyn.

"Hey, Sachs," he continued. "I'm partners with Schuster. Stop fucking with him, or you're gonna have trouble."

"I don't care who you are or who you're connected to. I told Schuster he's not allowed to be on my street hassling my customers. Tell him to take his complaints to court if he wants to collect his money."

"Be careful what you wish for, smart ass. You may get a visitor that will teach you a hard lesson."

"You know where to find me. Go fuck yourself." I slammed down the phone.

Within forty-five minutes Teddy Maggio and his nephew, Hank, showed up at my plant. It was a tense situation.

Three of my employees recognized the danger and

immediately walked out to the office to offer backup for me.

Maggio spoke first. "I'm tellin' you for the last time, Sachs. You don't know who you're fuckin' with. If you don't back off, believe me, brother, you are history. You're gonna end up with a major problem."

"Nothing's gonna change here. Bernie Schuster is out of line. And maybe you need to check to see who you're fuckin' with."

My answer seemed to take Maggio by surprise. He grunted in a scoffing manner, turned, and walked out the door.

My phone rang again about two hours later. It was Brooklyn.

Word gets around in the world of the Mob.

These calls never came directly from Johnny Green. He was too aware of FBI surveillance and wiretapping to be so foolish to allow his personal conversations to be recorded.

When speaking of Uncle John, maybe the correct adjective was "too smart."

"Stevie," the voice said. "Don't worry. This little problem you have is going away fast." The voice provided no details about how Uncle John could make this happen.

Experience had taught me not to ask.

A short time later, I received another call, this time from Joey D. "Steve," he said, "things are really happening. I spoke to Maggio. Can you meet with Maggio and Richie Lubben tomorrow morning at nine for breakfast at Frank's on 14th Street? I'll be there too. We have to settle this dispute before things get out of hand."

"Sure. I'll meet for breakfast. But not with Bernie Schuster. If he shows up, I'm going to beat the crap out of him."

Joey D laughed. "Nothing to worry about. Schuster won't be there," he said.

"All right. See you tomorrow at nine."

By the time I got to Frank's the next morning, Teddy Maggio,

Joey D, and Richie Lubben were already sitting in a booth.

I grabbed a chair, slid it over, and sat down on the outside of the booth. I saw a familiar face sitting on a stool at the end of the counter.

Who is he? I couldn't come up with his name.

We ordered breakfast and engaged in mostly small talk, nothing about Bernie Schuster. Maggio seemed much friendlier and relaxed. His antagonistic, aggressive attitude from the day before seemed to have vanished.

Was he trying to con me? Was I being set up?

The guy with the familiar face stood up from his seat at the counter and moved toward our booth. Suddenly, the bell went off in my brain.

Joey the Shooter, Maggio's nephew, a known hit man!

There was nothing I could do.

I had Bernie Schuster's .38 in my jacket pocket but had emptied the cartridges before I left my plant. I had totally relied on Brooklyn's statement that the problem with Maggio was going away.

Now what?

I swallowed hard.

Joey the Shooter stepped up behind me and leaned over, close to my ear. "Are you the Steve Sachs who was so close to Charlie A?" he whispered.

I turned and looked up at him. "Yes," I said.

I knew that Joey was a close associate of Charlie A and was known to take orders from him.

He stood up and looked over at Teddy Maggio. "Sorry, uncle, you're on your own here."

With that brief declaration, Joey the Shooter tapped his forehead in a playful salute to all of us at the booth, turned toward the exit, and walked out of the restaurant.

Teddy Maggio appeared stunned. He reached for his coffee, took a quick sip, and said nothing.

"I've got something for you," I said to him. I reached into my jacket, took out Bernie's .38, and handed it to Maggio. "It's empty, but you should tell Bernie this piece is gonna get him into trouble."

Maggio took the gun and nodded. "I'll tell Bernie he'd better cool it. From now on you won't see him showing up at your plant looking for the Greek. They'll have to work out their differences and leave us out of it."

After breakfast we shook hands all around.

For years to come, I did a lot of business with The Greek. We never had a problem. And I never ran into Bernie Schuster again.

As the voice on the Brooklyn call had predicted, the problem had gone away.

I was always amazed at the length of Uncle John's reach.

CHAPTER 26

Saving a Life from the Mob

IN THE MID-1980S I was looking to sign a larger distribution deal with Western Beef to expand our entire operation. I had been dealing with the Castellano family, who operated Western Beef, for more than twenty-five years and delivered to more than thirty of its stores weekly.

Topps was already big, but my goal was to make us even bigger.

Freddie Ruffino was also working for me and had a history of a half-assed relationship with Western Beef himself for their New York City supermarkets. I figured that Freddie and I could meet with the Castellanos to negotiate a good deal

I loved Freddie. He was a colorful human being—A hard worker and a streetwise guy, who like me, never took any shit from anyone and was not afraid to step into a fray when called upon to do the right thing. Freddie grew up in the Bronx and worked with Eatwell Sausage early in his career. He knew how to make contacts and was friendly with Billy and Frank Kissel, both of whom were eventually indicted for union racketeering. As he got older, his friendly and relaxed manner served him well as a salesman and helped him to make even more contacts with Mob members who were active in the meat industry. His ability to seamlessly navigate his way through Mob leaders and associates without ever being involved in illegal activities was clear testament to his engaging personality as well as his savvy in knowing how to avoid trouble.

Of course, it didn't hurt that he was also one of Charlie Anselmo's favorites. If you were fortunate enough to be close to Charlie A, you were the beneficiary of his personal security blanket. No one in the Mob dared to mess with one of Charlie A's guys.

I had met Freddie along the way at many meat-industry shows and developed a cordial relationship with him.

At one of my meetings with Uncle John, Freddie's name came up.

"Hey, Stevie," said Uncle John. "Freddie Ruffino is looking for a new job. How about you hire him to work with you at Topps?"

In my years of experience in dealing with the Mob, I had learned the subtlety of a request that was, in fact, an order. Fortunately, it was fairly easy for me to comply with this request.

The next day Freddie and I met in Little Italy for dinner. Within a week he was working for me. As it turned out he was exactly what I needed to control sales in the New York City supermarkets. He was a great employee, and over the years we also forged a very close relationship that extended to our wives. All of us were together on many social occasions.

In later years his wife developed terminal cancer. When I visited her in the hospital, she reached out and held my hand.

"Take care of my baby," she said, using the term she always reserved for Freddie.

I promised I would.

Freddie and I remained close friends for many years.

Freddie always carried a piece—a licensed .38 revolver.

"Personal protection," was his answer whenever I asked why he did.

Although I never saw him use his gun, I respected his right to carry it, and for sure there were times when I was glad he had it.

One Monday Freddie and I had a noon appointment at Western Beef Headquarters on Metropolitan Avenue. We were scheduled to meet with the head of the Castellano family and some of the younger sons who had gradually taken over a lot of the responsibilities of running their large operation.

Since this was an important business meeting, I wore an expensive suit that I had recently purchased at Barney's, an exclusive men's clothing store located downtown.

We entered Western Beef through the main door and announced ourselves to the receptionist who sat behind a Plexiglas window dividing the waiting area from the business office. She looked up with a big smile. "Yes," she said. "Mr. C has been delayed at another meeting, but he will return soon. Please have a seat."

Freddie and I looked at each other and grimaced while simultaneously shrugging our shoulders. We hated waiting, but what could we do?

A few minutes went by, and the main door opened. A young Black man, about twenty-five years old, stormed into the room. He was a big guy—about six foot three and weighed about 230 pounds. He rushed over to the window in front of the receptionist, spread his hands across the Plexiglas frame, leaned down to the talk hole in front of her, and began yelling. "Get the comptroller out here! I want my paycheck!" he screamed with a booming voice.

The receptionist recoiled instantly and pushed her chair away from the window. Shocked by the sudden intrusion, she sat motionless, appearing afraid to speak.

"Did you hear me?" the young man yelled. "I want the fuckin' payroll man out here now. This place owes me a paycheck."

In a conciliatory voice the receptionist leaned forward and held her hands out as if trying to console the intruder. "Now Stanley," she said, "you know Mr. Allan told you your check would be ready on Thursday."

"Fuck Mr. Allan! I want my fuckin' check now. They fired my ass last week for no good reason. Now they're holding my check? No fuckin' way!"

The young man appeared to be spinning out of control with every word.

She continued her attempts at calming him down. "Please, Stanley," she begged, "Don't be so upset. You're just going to get into trouble. You will get your check on Thursday as promised."

"Thursday? No! Not a fuckin' chance! I want my paycheck right now!"

Freddie and I sat silently watching the drama unfold.

Suddenly the young man pounded his fists on the Plexiglas window. The supporting frame rattled, and it appeared ready to separate from the soffit above.

The loud disturbance caused a bespectacled man to emerge from an office in the rear of the business area. He wore a white shirt and a necktie that dangled loosely from his open collar. He held a small stack of papers in his hands and had a bewildered look on his face. He appeared confused by the sudden, boisterous confrontation in what had been a peaceful work setting. As he walked closer, the man's face grew stern as he clearly recognized the source of the problem. "Stanley," he said, "you no longer work here, and if you don't leave immediately, I'm gonna call the cops."

Instead of frightening Stanley and causing him to back off,

the warning sent him into a further rage. He pounded on the Plexiglas window with even more violent blows. The noise was deafening. The entire room shook. "Mr. Allan," he yelled, "if you don't give me my paycheck, I'm gonna beat the shit out of you."

The door to the business office suddenly opened, and the receptionist and another woman ran out. They screamed as they ran through the waiting area and outside into the parking lot.

Stanley saw the open door to the business office and seized the opportunity to enter. In a flash he was inside and aggressively approaching the man he called Mr. Allan, who suddenly dropped his handful of papers to the floor.

Freddie and I looked at each other with the same quizzical expression.

Is this our fight? Do we get involved here?

Mr. Allan's stern face melted into a look of abject fear as he backed away from the stalking Stanley.

Stanley grabbed him by the collar and threw him up against a metal file cabinet. "I want my fuckin' paycheck now," he yelled. The file cabinet slammed against the wall and then came crashing down onto a desk. A half-filled mug of coffee shattered into dozens of pieces. The coffee splattered everywhere. Files and folders were strewn all over the floor.

I got up from my chair and made a move toward the business office.

Freddie's arm reached out and grabbed me. "No, boss, you're still on six-month probation for that problem in New Jersey. You can't get involved in this. Let me take care of it." He reached behind his back, removed the .38 from his belt holster, and handed it to me. "Here," he said. "Hold my piece. I'm going in."

Freddie was five feet ten inches tall and physically fit, but as he ran into the business office, I had the feeling that he was no match for that huge kid.

I stood in the waiting room and watched through the window. Stanley had a firm grasp of Mr. Allan's neck and was slamming him against the wall.

Two other men had come out of the rear offices but were of no use. They yelled "Stop it! Let him go!" But they were clearly afraid to mix it up with the imposing Stanley and stood far enough away, out of his reach.

Freddie bolted into the room and surprised Stanley, tackling him from behind with a solid shoulder hit to his lower back. Stanley's grasp on Mr. Allan loosened and then let go as Freddie brought him down to the floor.

The two men grappled on the floor for a few minutes, and it seemed that Freddie had achieved a decisive advantage.

Mr. Allan struggled to his feet, and, almost dazed, retreated to a rear office instead of staying nearby to assist Freddie.

Suddenly Freddie let out a loud scream.

He grabbed at his hand and rolled away from Stanley.

Freddie quickly got up on his feet and made his way out toward me in the waiting room. He cradled his right hand as he approached. "The prick broke my thumb. I had to get out of there."

I handed his .38 back to him. "Can you use this with your left hand?" I asked.

Freddie looked stunned. "Yeah, if I was forced to." He paused for a second and then looked straight into my eyes in disbelief. "You want me to shoot this kid?"

"Well, only if I can't get him under control and it looks like he might kill me or someone else in there."

Freddie's mouth dropped open but said nothing as I turned and ran into the office.

The other two men passed me as they escaped from the building.

By this time, Mr. Allan had locked himself into a rear office.

Stanley had picked up a straight back chair and began slamming it against the door, screaming expletives and threatening to kill Mr. Allan.

The scene was pure bedlam.

"Stanley!" I shouted.

He turned to look at me.

I calmly walked toward him.

"Relax, son," I said. "You don't know what you're doing here."

He cut me off before I could say another word. "I want my fuckin' paycheck. These bastards owe me. I want my money. I earned it."

I moved closer to him. "Listen, son. You can't come in here and destroy this office. Let's talk about this."

He backed away and moved toward the farther wall.

Mr. Allan had evidently heard our conversation and assumed that the crisis had been resolved. The knob to his office door turned. Mr. Allan quickly stepped out and made a desperate move to escape toward the exit.

Stanley lunged toward him in another attempt to grab him by the neck.

Mr. Allan eluded his hands and frantically darted out of the office.

Sensing Stanley's distraction, I stepped forward and hit him with a groin shot that brought him down to his knees.

Stanley let out a painful groan and gasped for air.

I leaned over, grabbed him by the head and took him down to the floor with a powerful headlock. I pushed his back and shoulders up against the wall, totally immobilizing his upper body.

Stanley flailed his legs uselessly, trying to kick me, but I had neutralized his leverage.

I squeezed his neck harder.

He continued to resist my efforts. His face reddened. Large beads of perspiration rolled off his forehead. Blood trickled down his face from a cut above his right eye.

I leaned down toward his face.

Our faces were inches apart as I spoke calmly to him. "Listen carefully, Stanley. Within a few minutes some men will be arriving here. You may think they simply run a meat business, but they do much more than that. If you continue to destroy this office, these men will kill you. Then they will cut your body up into pieces and dump it in a landfill where no one will ever find it. Your family will never know what happened to you. You will just disappear."

Stanley's eyes widened.

I continued to speak to him. "Stanley, I don't want to hurt you, but I will have no say in what happens to you if you continue your rampage when these men come back. You need to stop fighting, get up, and let me walk you out of here. If you don't, you're a dead man." I slowly relaxed my vice-like grip around his head. I leaned back and released the pressure on his shoulders.

Stanley continued to stare at me. His muscles, which had been totally flexed, eased—no resistance whatsoever.

He nodded slowly.

My message had been clear. I knew he understood what I had just told him.

We heard voices from the outer office.

Peter Castellano and his crew walked in and stopped dead in their tracks at the scene of utter destruction before them.

"What the fuck!" said Joey the Notch, one of Peter's henchmen.

Joey glared at Stanley, stepped forward, and reached back, preparing to punch him on the left side of his face.

I quickly stepped between them and kept Joey from swinging. "We're okay here," I said. "Just a big misunderstanding. Everything's all settled. Stanley won't be coming back here again. Mr. Allan is mailing Stanley's check to him on Thursday."

Peter C gave me a confused look. He looked down at my pants, which had a huge rip in one of the legs. My expensive wristwatch lay broken on the floor.

He glanced up at Stanley.

Stanley nodded. "That's right, Mr. C," he said. "I won't be comin' back here again."

Peter C looked over to me. "Just get him the hell out of here. We have to talk business."

I took Stanley by the arm and walked him outside.

We said nothing.

When we got out to the parking lot, he turned toward me with a hostile look. "You weren't foolin' with me, were you? Those guys would really kill me?"

"In a heartbeat."

He waved his arms in frustration. "But I was just pissed at them, man. They fired me. I needed the money today. I couldn't wait."

"Did you see that guy who came in with Peter C?

"Yeah. I've seen him around. That guy they call Joey the Notch?"

"You know how he got his nickname?"

"No."

"He has notches on his gun handle for every man he's killed."

Stanley's mouth dropped open.

"They don't let anyone beat them, Stanley," I said, "especially the way you tried. Just walk away, kid. Cash your check when you get it and move on."

Stanley turned toward the street and began walking. Then he stopped and looked back to me. "Thanks, man."

I nodded.

He smiled. "You're a tough sonovabitch for an older guy."

"Have to be, if I'm going to deal with those guys."

He laughed. He continued walking and then disappeared around the corner.

I turned and walked back into the building.

A few minutes later Freddie and I sat down with the brass at Western Beef in its plush private office to discuss the framework of a new deal.

Because of the physical stress and the energy I had expended trying to subdue Stanley, I was a mess. The right leg on my pants was ripped from the knee all the way down to the ankle. My face had several scratches and small ripples of blood trickled down from my forehead. My shirt had become soaked with perspiration. I grabbed a tissue from a box on the conference table and dabbed at the scratches.

Peter Castellano looked at me for a few seconds and seemed to assess the damage I had sustained. I was expecting him to follow up with some words of consolation for my condition or at least some acknowledgment or appreciation for what I had done to subdue the out-of-control young man who had terrorized his staff.

But he said nothing. He glanced down at some papers on the conference table and then looked up at me. "You want a glass of water, Steve, before we talk business?" he asked.

A lousy glass of water? After what I did for you? I almost laughed in his face but managed to contain myself.

It became a contentious meeting. They were totally inflexible on their pricing, and we couldn't agree. They also seemed oblivious to the disruptive scenario that had played out less than half an hour earlier in their office, a scenario in which I had saved them from themselves, preventing them from rubbing out a disgruntled former employee and having to deal with the criminal fallout, a crime of which their own employees could be witnesses for the prosecution as the last persons to see the former employee alive.

All this after I had provided twenty-five years of loyalty and friendship?

How was it possible?

Instead, Peter C. and his crew were consumed with driving a hard, unrealistic deal to make greater profits for themselves at the expense of my company.

The negotiations went nowhere.

After listening to their proclamations, I sat quietly, having made my decision: I was finished with Western Beef. I got up from my seat.

Freddie followed my lead.

"Thanks, Peter," I said. "Looks like this won't work for us."

Freddie and I shook hands with Peter C and his underlings and walked out of the office.

I went back to my sales staff and gave them the edict: we needed new accounts to replace those we had with Western Beef.

Within three weeks our new accounts brought in more money than our previous deal with Western Beef.

I eventually bought a new suit and an expensive wristwatch.

CHAPTER 27

Las Vegas

IN THE EARLY 1990s we were operating our Topps Meat plant in Elizabeth, New Jersey. Our business kept growing, and I had built the retail division into a national brand. Anthony wanted no part of the retail supermarket portion and instead concentrated on wholesale foods sales. We were growing so fast that we had some of the biggest accounts in the entire wholesale industry. They included Roma Foods, U.S. Foods, and the Performance Food Group.

Despite all this success, we were ambitious and had big plans to expand even further. At this same time my life had also taken a more personal and positive turn. Although an early marriage produced two beautiful children who have always been the focus of my love and admiration, I wasn't truly happy until this point in my life when I met and married the woman with whom I have shared the rest of my life.

During this time, I continued to have close personal ties with the Mob but was comfortable in knowing that it was an arm's-length relationship when it came to my business.

But then I got a phone call from Brooklyn.

I was summoned to a meeting on an important matter. Nothing else was said, and I knew enough not to ask for further details.

As usual I drove to a fast-food location—this time a McDonald's—parked my car, walked in, ordered a cup of coffee, and sat down in a booth.

Several minutes later a young guy I had never seen before sat down in the booth across from me. He looked around at the customers in line and the few people sitting at tables. Seeming satisfied that no one was paying attention, he looked over and made eye contact with me. "Take your time. Finish your coffee," he said. "We have a few minutes."

I took a couple of gulps and pushed my cup aside. "I'm all set," I said.

"Black Chrysler on the left side of the lot. Give me a minute before you come out."

I just nodded and watched as he casually got up and walked out the door.

These encounters always fascinated me because of the Mob's extreme attention to detail—persistent paranoia—when it came to these meetings. Mob members were consumed with fear that they were under constant surveillance and that the Feds could pressure anyone with whom they met to turn state's evidence and testify against them.

My driver got me to the plumbing shop in time for lunch. The special for the day was meatballs and pasta.

Uncle John greeted me with his usual enthusiasm. "Stevie! How good to see you. I hear your business is doing great."

After a few pleasantries, we filled our plates and sat down at the usual table for two, which was how Uncle John liked to do business—one on one; "*hombre* to *hombre*."

His agenda for the day was Las Vegas.

"Stevie, I know a guy—Brooklyn guy—in Las Vegas. His name is Mr. Vincent."

"Is that his first name or last?" I asked.

"Don't worry; just Mr. Vincent is all you need to know for now."

I took another mouthful of pasta and waited for the story to unfold with more details. I had the distinct feeling that I would be boarding an airplane for Vegas very soon.

"This guy," he continued, "this guy is in control of purchasing the meat and seafood for eight large hotels on the Strip. I want you to go to Vegas and meet with him. See what kind of offer he can make. Maybe you want to go partners with us. This could be a very big deal."

I put my fork down and took a drink of Coke from the can. I turned my chair so I could look straight into his eyes. "Uncle John, anything I sell into Vegas has to be through legitimate brokerage firms at numbers that work for everybody."

He nodded. "I understand," he said.

"And I'll need to take my partner, Joey D's son Anthony, with me. He deals with this type of large-scale purchase and will handle the actual sale presentation to Mr. Vincent."

Uncle John just shrugged and offered a gentle smile. "Stevie, I know you'll do the right thing."

With that the business portion of our meeting was over. We finished eating, and within half an hour, I was on my way back to McDonald's to pick up my van.

Three days later Anthony and I arrived in Las Vegas. We checked into Caesar's Palace at two p.m. and waited for our phone contact.

Nothing.

Finally, after we had dinner, we received a call from a man stating that we would be picked up at eight p.m. At eight o'clock sharp a black limo pulled up to the entrance of Caesar's Palace. The driver got out and held a sign that read "Steve."

We got into the limo and were driven to a club just outside

the Strip. The club had a large sign over the entrance—Crazy Horse Too. The driver opened the rear doors of the limo and told us to go inside, where our contact would meet us. He motioned toward a guy who stood by a door collecting entry fees from a long line of men waiting to enter.

The doorman looked over, nodded to the driver, and waved us toward him.

We paid nothing to get in.

We walked into a dark nightclub with dozens of small tables placed around a centered stage with bright psychedelic lights in the background. Naked young women danced on the stage, while topless waitresses walked through the crowd of onlookers serving drinks.

A manager walked over to us and asked, "Are you here to meet someone?"

"Mr. Vincent," I said.

He nodded and escorted us to a booth occupied by a short gray-haired man who looked to be in his sixties.

"Welcome," he said. "You must be Steve."

"I am. And you must be Mr. Vincent. This is my junior partner, Anthony."

We sat down and ordered drinks. The conversation was light and cordial.

Finally, I asked, "Is Vincent your last name or your first?"

"Just Mr. Vincent will do," he replied.

I grasped the picture and didn't follow up with any other questions about his name. Neither the Mob nor this guy was interested in revealing his identity at that time.

"I control all the meat purchases for eight of the largest hotels on the Strip," he said. He continued with a detailed description of the items he would purchase from us and the brokerage rate he would charge for his services.

I listened intently but noticed that Anthony's eyes kept drifting toward the naked dancers on the stage. I slapped him on the back of the head to focus his attention to the business discussion at our table.

We all laughed.

Our laughter broke the tension at the table, and the conversation continued in an open and friendly manner. At the end of our discussion, we had a couple of drinks, shook hands, and Anthony and I left the nightclub. We took a cab back to our hotel.

"Stevie, this is a big deal. We have to jump on it," said Anthony.

I looked over at him and shook my head.

"The numbers don't work," I said. "Between the transportation costs and the high brokerage fee he's asking for, there's nothing left for us."

"So you're going to turn it down?"

"I think so."

"How are you going to explain that to Uncle John?"

"I haven't figured that out yet."

Once again, I had a lot to think about before I met with Uncle John.

A few days later we were back in New York. I set up the meeting and rode to the plumbing shop via my usual mode of transportation.

In my experience with the Mob I had learned that its members didn't accept rejection very graciously. If they had their minds made up about taking over a business, they always got their way, either by paying the price or through the exertion of brute force. At other times they simply applied subtle pressure—never an overt threat, rather one that was implied—thereby making a person think twice about deciding against their recommendation.

I knew that Uncle John must have had a financial interest in this deal; otherwise, why would he bother getting involved in meat shipments to Las Vegas? A kickback from the brokerage fee was the logical source. but how could I tell him to eliminate his fee?

I arrived at the plumbing shop and was escorted to the back office. It was a bit early for lunch, so Uncle John and I sipped cappuccino and snacked on some delicious biscotti from the local Italian bakery.

Uncle John wasted no time cutting to the chase. "What do you think of Mr. Vincent's offer?" he asked.

"It's certainly a big deal, very high volume, but there's no profit there," I said.

"No profit? How come?"

"Transportation of that quantity of meat will be too expensive. And the brokerage fee is too high. The only other way to lower the overhead is to lower the quality of the meat, and I'm not about to do that. My reputation in this industry is based on a high-quality product. If I start selling inferior meat, I'm done."

"So, what are you saying?"

"No deal."

He paused.

"Are you sure? This could mean a lot of money to us."

"I understand, but the deal has no margin for me. No profit. I can't occupy production time for a contract that has nothing for me."

"Did you tell Mr. Vincent that?"

"No. I wanted to tell you first."

Uncle John sat quietly, nodding as he looked across at me, processing the information I had just presented. Then he spoke. "Stevie, you're an honest man. I trust you. If you say no deal, then I know the deal doesn't work for everybody. I'll let Mr.

Vincent know that he has to find a different supplier."

We sat and talked for a while and enjoyed another cup of cappuccino.

He then called for my driver, and I was escorted out of the office.

As I left the plumbing shop, I realized that in my long relationship with the Mob, I may have just dodged a bullet.

CHAPTER 28

After Las Vegas: The Old Homestead

MY PARTNER, JOEY D, and his son Anthony understood why I had to turn down the Las Vegas deal; nevertheless, they were disappointed. Joey D in particular was looking to expand his other business, Demar Pork—a pork, beef, and poultry distribution company—into supermarkets in New York.

I felt I owed it to him to offer my help. I knew that the Mob had its hooks into many supermarkets in New York and that any such deal had to go through the Mob. The best way for me to navigate that channel was to go through Uncle John.

I spoke to Uncle John and provided all of the details about Demar Pork and Joey D's interest in expanding his distribution into supermarkets.

Even though I had just turned down his Las Vegas deal, Uncle John continued to treat me like I was part of his family. He set up a meeting with several Mob associates who had major influence over New York City's larger supermarket chains. The meeting took place at the world-famous Old Homestead Steak Restaurant on 14th Street and 9th Avenue.

Uncle John knew the reputations of the characters who

would meet me. They were a tough bunch that wanted things their way. Since he was always concerned about my safety, unbeknownst to me, he asked Sonny P to show up at the restaurant in case the discussion got out of hand.

I had some misgivings myself, so I asked Freddie Ruffino to come along and wait outside. I knew that Freddie would be carrying his piece.

When I got to the restaurant I was escorted to an area in the back that had a large upholstered booth. Two older men in their seventies whom I didn't know were sitting there with two people I knew very well—Jimmy Blue Eyes of the Bonanno crew and Johnny Spitface of the Anselmo family.

Another man sat across from them, a man I knew all too well and a person for whom I had a strong dislike: John "Machine Gun" Pandolfi. I gave him that nickname because he was such a fast talker. Words came out of his mouth like rapid fire. He also earned the nickname because he always stored some weapons in the trunk of his car: handguns, rifles, and even an automatic rifle.

John and I glared at each other.

My best guess was that he had come to this meeting "packing," probably one of his many small handguns. After all, in many ways I was one of his main competitors. Eliminate me and an entire new market would open up for him.

An air of tension suddenly pervaded the room.

I sat down in the booth and looked around the table. *Was it possible that I had just walked into a trap of my own making?*

Just then a waiter walked by to bring drinks to another table. I glanced up at him quickly and then had to be careful not to overreact by looking at him again. It was Sonny P, wearing a waiter's uniform and walking around delivering drinks like he always worked there. (I later found out that his cousin was a maître d' at Old Homestead and arranged for him to be undercover.)

I knew that Sonny P always "carried." I thought, *Good Ol' Uncle John—taking care of one of "his boys."*

Knowing that I had plenty of backup, I relaxed and spoke first. "My partner, Joey D, is looking to expand his pork distribution business—" I started.

"Save it!" Pandolfi snapped. "Johnny Green already gave us the details."

I stopped and gave Pandolfi a look.

"Listen," he said. "Let's get something straight here. If you do business with us, you do it on our terms."

I looked at him calmly, with no expression. "And just what are your terms?" I asked.

"Cash brokerage at seven percent."

I shook my head. "No cash brokerage, only legitimate payment by check is the game plan here. And your brokerage fee is way out of line."

Pandolfi leaned forward from his seat, trying to get nose to nose with me. "If you don't play ball with me, I'll make sure your fuckin' Topps line of meat will be discontinued in every supermarket in New York. I can bury your fuckin' company, and you know it."

I looked at the two older Mob men and could tell they were watching very carefully for my response. I turned to Pandolfi. "With all due respect to these two other gentlemen, don't ever threaten me again. Never! If you do, I will cut the cost of my Topps products below the competition. The customer traffic in your stores will come to a standstill. You talk "bury?" Let me tell you something. I will bury your stores with prices so low they can't possibly match them, because they're paying such overinflated fees to you."

Pandolfi's eyes grew wide and his face was filled with rage. It appeared that he was ready to reach across the table, grab me by the collar, and punch me.

The two henchmen that flanked him looked at each other.

Had they received their cue to join Pandolfi and teach me a lesson?

The tension in the room ratcheted up another notch.

Just then Sonny P walked by and leaned against the back wall about twenty feet away. His eyes were fixed on our booth and his waiter's jacket was unbuttoned to reveal a bulging object on his right hip.

Freddie Ruffino also entered the room and sat down at a table diagonally across from our booth. He slowly unzipped his black leather jacket in an obvious manner to display a shoulder strap supporting the holster of his .38.

The appearance of both men, obviously carrying firearms, garnered the immediate attention of everyone seated at the booth. The balance of power had suddenly shifted dramatically in my favor.

Jimmy Blue Eyes sensed the gravity of the situation. Ever the peacemaker, he held his hand out toward Pandolfi in a "stop" gesture. "Relax, John. Settle down here," he said. "Stevie is a good friend."

Aware that the deck was stacked against him and that his usual aggressive approach wasn't going to work, Pandolfi leaned back in his seat and waved off Jimmy's hand in an obvious sign of reluctant surrender.

The booth was quiet for a few seconds.

"Well," I said. "I want to thank you guys for getting together. We all have some things to think over. I'll get back to Johnny within a week with our final answer unless I hear from you sooner with a better offer."

I shook hands with Jimmy Blue Eyes and got up from my seat at the booth.

Sonny P buttoned his waiter's jacket and walked toward the kitchen.

Freddie stood warily at attention, jacket still unzipped, waiting for me to join him. We left the restaurant together and drove back to our plant in Elizabeth, New Jersey.

Joey D and I discussed the offer at length and came to a mutual conclusion that it was not possible for us to conduct a legitimate business in the manner offered to us.

Two weeks later Sonny P and I met Uncle John for dinner in his favorite Italian restaurant in Brooklyn. We had three courses of delicious food and several bottles of great Italian wine. We also teased Sonny P about his audition for a new career as a waiter.

Uncle John laughed like hell.

When the dinner was over, Uncle John insisted on picking up the dinner check, which was his traditional pleasure—taking care of his boys.

Years later, after I had retired and moved to Florida, the word eventually came that several weeks earlier Uncle John had died of heart failure. He was in his late eighties. His passing was without fanfare. There was no mention in the obituaries of the New York newspapers about his alleged Mob connections. After all, he had never been arrested or indicted and never served prison time for any crime. Thus he had successfully conducted his long and vitally important career for the Mob by flying completely under the radar of the FBI and other government agencies that were surveilling the Mob.

I was filled with sadness that I had not had the opportunity to attend his funeral and pay my respects to his family.

I loved that old guy.

CHAPTER 29

Turkeys

JUST AFTER LABOR Day in September 2001, the fast-paced, high-demand summer hamburger season was slowing down for our supermarket customers. At Topps we almost welcomed the downtime to relax a little.

Joey came into the office around ten in the morning. Joey drove a big Lincoln, and since we were not expecting any deliveries that morning, he pulled it into the truck receiving area, where it was just underneath the open overhead steel door.

We sat around the office talking about business and sports and making plans to go to Atlantic City with our wives for the weekend. Anthony was downstairs on the receiving platform talking to the head of our meat receiving department.

It was a low-stress day.

Late in the morning a group of neighborhood black kids about fourteen years old walked by Topps during a school lunch break. One of the bigger kids decided to be a wise guy. He ran over to the side of the garage door and pressed the button to close the overhead door.

Anthony saw what was happening and rushed over to stop the door before it crashed into the roof of his father's car. He also grabbed the kid by the left arm as he tried to run away.

The kid swung wildly at Anthony and struck him on the side of the face with a glancing blow.

Anthony pushed the kid down to the sidewalk but had lost control of the left arm.

The kid bolted up to his feet and ran off before Anthony could stop him.

Within fifteen minutes a large group of Haitians, Jamaicans, and African Americans had gathered in front of our plant.

I was upstairs in my office and heard loud voices yelling outside.

One of my secretaries called up to me, "Steve, you need to come down here fast!"

I grabbed my "38th Street bat" and ran downstairs and out to the street.

Anthony stood in front of the angry group trying to reason with a woman who was evidently the kid's mother. Their discussion had become heated.

"You had no right to shove my child down to the ground and hurt his head," she yelled.

The kid stepped up next to her and pointed to a bruise on his forehead.

"He was trying to damage that car," said Anthony, pointing over to the Lincoln.

"I don't see any damage on that car," she screamed.

Our night watchman, Henry, an African American man himself and an employee for nearly thirty years, tried to step in and reason with the mother, but he was getting nowhere.

The crowd grew angrier and a few of the men approached Anthony.

Henry looked over to me and motioned with his head that I had to intervene.

I cupped my bat between my palm and armpit and walked

into the middle of the crowd. "All right, everybody," I said quietly. "Everybody needs to calm down, or this situation is going to get really ugly."

Several of the bigger men in the group moved toward me. Their faces bore a strained, defiant look.

I stepped toward the largest man in the group.

He looked at me with a scowl.

"Your crowd has us outnumbered and will eventually take me down, maybe even kill me," I said, "but before I go down, you're gonna have to deal with a beating from this bat, and not many guys have come through a beating like that in good shape." I stood defiantly, but not with a threatening appearance. My bat remained cradled in my arm.

The man blinked.

The crowd grew quiet.

Just then the sound of police sirens filled the air. Six Elizabeth, New Jersey, squad cars pulled up. A sergeant opened his door and yelled over to me, "Steve, is everything okay here?"

The crowd immediately began to back away and disperse.

"Under control," I said. "Everything is under control."

I walked over to the kid's mother. "I'm sorry for what happened here, but if that steel door had hit the roof of that car, there could have been thousands of dollars of damage. You wouldn't want your son to get in trouble or have to be responsible for the repairs."

She looked over to her son.

The kid turned away, seemingly embarrassed by the revelation of the facts of the incident.

Henry stepped forward toward the mother. "Steve is a good person; you can trust him," he said. "He wouldn't want your boy to get in trouble."

She looked up and extended her hand to me.

We shook hands.

Two months later, in early November, Anthony bought one hundred turkeys. We packed them into our truck and delivered them to our neighbors on the street—the same group that had protested in front of our plant. At every stop we were greeted with smiles and happy faces.

I was thrilled to see their reactions.

It was a great Thanksgiving.

We never had trouble or acts of vandalism at Topps again.

By 2003 Topps Meat Company had grown to be one of the largest manufacturers of retail frozen hamburger patties in the United States. I was proud of this accomplishment, not only because of the financial rewards I had gained as a co-owner, but also because of the quality of the product we distributed. We never cut corners to make a bigger profit, and we always maintained stringent production standards to ensure that our hamburger meat was safe for the consumer.

Joey D. and I achieved success with Topps despite union intrusions, interference from the Mob, and generalized corruption within the meat industry. We resisted all these negative influences and never wavered in our insistence on running a legitimate business.

Later that year I was approached by a large financial firm with an offer to buy Topps. The offer included an option for a complete cash buyout or a partial buyout that would allow me to share in the future profits of the company. Although I recognized the long-term benefits of the second option, the prospects of taking orders on operational matters from a new owner was not appealing to me. I knew I was leaving money on the table, but I decided to accept the complete buyout and move on to retirement. Joey D. stepped back from day-to-day operations but retained an investor position in the new company.

In October 2007, Topps made headlines when the United States Department of Agriculture investigated reports of E. coli infections associated with hamburger meat sold to supermarkets by the Topps Meat Company of Elizabeth, New Jersey. Within weeks more than thirty people in eight states had developed E. coli infections that matched the strain of E. coli found in Topps hamburger patties. (6)

Fortunately, there were no fatalities, but the reputation of Topps suffered an instant death.

In order to comply with government regulations and simultaneously regain the confidence of the public, Topps issued a recall for 21.7 million pounds of hamburger—nearly a year's worth of production. However, the impact of the enormous recall had a devastating effect on Topps's financial position.

Despite all efforts, the reputation of the company could not be resurrected. A few weeks later, Topps went out of business. Eighty-seven employees lost their jobs.

I watched this news from afar with a host of varying emotions: shock that the new owners had disregarded our intense safety standards in order to improve their bottom line; disappointment that many of my longtime employees—wonderful, loyal people, I had hired years earlier—were now out of work; but thankful that I had made the right decision to retire and not remain partners with the new owners.

Topps Meat Company had been in business for sixty-seven years.

The people who bought us out killed it in four years.

Epilogue

MOST OF MY friends from my early life who have been mentioned in this book are gone. Many have died, either by natural causes or assassination. Others are living under assumed names or as part of the witness protection program. Many spent time in prison for a wide variety of crimes, including loan sharking, racketeering, income tax evasion, and even authorizing or committing murder. Some of them died in prison while serving a sentence for these crimes, among others.

I never stood in judgment of their private lives outside of our friendship. Those things were their business; I had my own life. Our lives intersected on the common ground of our friendship—in several cases, a friendship of nearly fifty years.

The basis of my relationship with members of the Mob was trust. I trusted them, and they trusted me. None of the favors I did for them were illegal, and I never accepted financial compensation for any favor or information I gathered on their behalf.

These men respected my determination to conduct my life and my business in a totally legitimate manner. They never tried to lure me into any of their illegal activities and never asked me to compromise my values. In return I respected their privacy regarding all of their business matters, even though I knew that many were nefarious, to say the least.

I heard rumors and read newspaper accounts by investigative journalists who chronicled the criminal extent of the Mob, particularly the Mafia families in New York. Some of these stories mentioned the names of my friends and detailed the expansive nature of their corrupt criminal enterprise. Although I read these reports with interest, I never discussed them with my friends in the Mob. Likewise, they never discussed these stories with me or rebutted the information in my presence.

Looking back on those times, I now understand that in many ways my friends were trying to protect not only me, but also themselves. If they had told me the details of their illegal activities, the name of a person they had beaten or assassinated, or the name of a police officer or politician they had bribed, the FBI could have eventually coerced me to provide this information and testify against them. If I perjured myself or refused to testify, another indicted Mob associate seeking a plea bargain could have corroborated my involvement. If so, I could have gone to prison.

As it stands now, because my friends were so determined to protect me, I never witnessed any crime and have no specific testimony to offer.

What I admired the most about my friends in the Mob was their dedication to their families. While they were under constant surveillance from the FBI and other government agencies, they understood that their days of illegal activities were numbered, either by incarceration or assassination by a fellow Mob family seeking to take over a territory. When this scenario transformed from a possibility to inevitability, their focus was centered on protecting their families. As a result, they worked tirelessly to set up legitimate business opportunities for their wives and children.

Few of the Mob bosses or associates had ever attended college. Some had never graduated from high school, but they encouraged their children to go to college and pursue postgraduate education so that they could obtain the credentials necessary to pursue a career as a business entrepreneur, as an attorney, or as a member of the health professions.

Many of the children and grandchildren of Mob associates are now thriving in professional careers or as owners of restaurant chains, as well as various other completely legitimate business enterprises.

I also admired the bond of loyalty, honor, and respect that was part of the mantra of the Mob. If a *capo*, a made-man, or an associate was dying as a result of a terminal disease, the head of the family visited the individual and asked if he had any final wishes. Almost always, the wish was very straightforward: "Take care of my family."

The head of the family then gave his word that the request would be honored. To the best of my knowledge, this commitment was never broken. The stories that I heard about such instances had a definite impact on me.

When my partner Joey D'urso was diagnosed with stage four pancreatic cancer, he had less than four months to live. On his deathbed, in a halting voice barely able to speak, Joey asked me to look out for his son, Anthony.

I clasped Joey's hand and managed to fight back my own tears. "I promise to be like a second father to Anthony and always treat him as my own son." I consider that promise to be a vow that I am bound to keep for the rest of my life. I guess one could say it was a lesson I learned from my friends in the Mob.

Since that time, my relationship with Anthony has grown and become only stronger each year. He is a wonderful young man.

Many times, we reminisce and laugh—and admittedly, sometimes cry—when we talk of the times we had when the three of us were together.

Acknowledgments

The authors are indebted to the following people who offered their assistance during the writing and completion of the final draft of this manuscript:

Our preview readers: Kristen Rzezuski; Phyllis Oblas; Diane Beane; Maire Mason of Univision and her husband, John Coyne; Joe Bellargo; Robin Boretti; and retired City of Yonkers police officer, Michael DelPeschio. Thank you for the many hours you devoted to reading and critiquing our early drafts.

Ronney O'Donnell, who served as our final editor and whose painstaking, meticulous approach always managed to ferret out the mistake that everyone else missed.

References

1. en.wikipedia.org/wiki/The Tombs
2. En.wikipedia.org/wiki/Ringolevio
3. *The Edge: Organized Crime, Business and Labor Unions. Report to the resident and Attorney General.* May 1986. page 216.
4. *The Edge: Organized Crime, Business and Labor Unions. Report to the President and Attorney General.* May 1986, page 211.
5. *Vicious Circles: The Mafia in the Marketplace.* W.W. Norton & Company, 1979. Pages 16-19, 21-23
6. FoxNews.com/story/topps-meat-company-shutters-business. October 5, 2007

CPSIA information can be obtained
at www.ICGtesting.com
Printed in the USA
BVHW032014200222
629604BV00005B/131